IT CAN HAPPEN TO ANYBODY!

by

RUSSELL BIXLER

Dedicated to the members of the Pittsburgh Church of the Brethren, who for more than ten years have put up with a young pastor's growing pains.

Preface

I remember the days when Russell Bixler came to class with that frustrated look all over his face. I saw the look begin to change.

Since then I have seen Russell's joy in the ministry, when many other ministers are frustrated to despair.

I believe in God the Father, in Jesus Christ His Revelation, and in the Holy Spirit through whom He is now present in our lives and in our midst.

I am not afraid of the work of the Holy Spirit in anyone's life, because I trust God the Father, Son and Holy Spirit. We are advised to honor our leaders and *imitate their faith,* which is in Jesus Christ, the same yesterday and today and for ever (Heb. 13:8).

Listen carefully to what Russell has to tell. Commit your life without reserve to the same Lord, and God's greatest blessing will be yours also.

In His Name,
Anna B. Mow

Dr. Anna B. Mow, former missionary to India, later Professor of Christian Education at Bethany

Theological Seminary, Chicago, and popular leader
of retreats and conferences, is the author of *Say
"Yes" to Life, Your Child, Going Steady with God*
and *Your Teenager and You,* published by Zonder-
van, and *Who's Afraid of Birthdays?* and *The Se-
cret of Married Love,* published by Lippincott.

Introduction

Port Allegany, Pa.

After months of gentle nudging, God has finally led me here to Ellie Armstrong's Port Motel. Nearly a year ago the Lord began to tell me that I was to take one week of vacation, not for our family, but just for Him and me. Some time later He put it in my heart to hold our "retreat" here in Port Allegany. "But, Lord! That's so far away! And a motel is expensive!"

Several years ago I had resolved—not too firmly—to stop arguing with "the Boss." I had lost every argument anyhow. As you can see, He won this one too. Then He began to tell me what I was to do here. First, it was to be a time of fellowship with Jesus and an opportunity to be taught by the Holy Spirit. Beyond this the instructions were not yet clear. Then about a month ago He told me that together we would write *our* story.

How silly that sounded! My life hasn't been as dramatic as that of Paul, nor Augustine, Francis of Assisi, Billy Bray or any number of contemporary figures. My life, I protested, is a story of failure. Human failure. "That is correct," spoke that

7

quiet familiar voice. "Human failure it is. But combined with *My* success, *your* human failure makes *our* story all the more miraculous." Still, I felt a lack of conviction.

Last Tuesday I stopped by to see a business-man-friend about a certain matter. As I started to leave he said, "Sit down a minute, Russ." I turned back to listen. "Why don't you write your testimony? You write it, and we'll publish it."

I nearly choked getting the answer out: "That's exactly what the Lord told me to do!"

Thursday evening we went to visit and pray with some friends who had been involved in a car accident. In the midst of the small talk Marian turned abruptly and gushed, quite out of context of the conversation, "Russ, you should write a book!"

So here I am—or rather, here we are—writing our story together. Even as my mind hurries into the first chapter, the pain and the hurt begin to rise in my heart, for it is a chronicle of human failure.

Perhaps you can identify with the story as you read.

CONTENTS

I. *Born in Fear and Frustration*

Fear and frustration indeed! I was just old
enough to remember my hard-working father sitting in a chair of frustration, his right arm in a
sling. A year-and-a-half of enforced idleness due
to a badly-injured shoulder ended in the deepest
gloom of the Great Depression, when it seemed that
everybody was experiencing enforced idleness.

Dad was different. He was accustomed to creat-
ing his own opportunities. We moved from Boston
to the little town of Westminster, Maryland, where
Dad (and the bank) owned a small piece of prop-
erty. The quarters were cramped, but we ate three
meals a day; and Dad developed a new business
which provided a narrow margin of living for his
growing family.

But their oldest child had been born scared.
Both parents had come from broken homes. Dad had
been taken out of school at the age of nine to earn
his own living; on the other side of the family my
grandmother had died when Mother was only four.
Understandably, Dad saw life materialistically and
Mother was fearful and lonely. I inherited a heart-
ful from both. Insecurity was all I ever felt.

Studies came rather easy: they tell me I have a

high I.Q. But on the basis of accomplishments I was consistently underachieving my potential. I had big ambitions—perhaps only to seem pleasing to Dad—yet at night I would repeatedly dream that I was falling, ever falling from crumbling mountain tops. Any psychologist can explain the dreams: great ambition, little fulfillment. The sudden midnight trembling and perspiring is a most vivid memory.

"What do you want to be, Russell?"

My stock answer was, "A doctor."

"Why a doctor?"

"Because doctors make lots of money."

In my early teens there began to develop a streak of idealism which has ever since affected my life, leading me to shift my goals to the political field. Surely politics offered the greatest possibility for doing the most good. But this meant great disappointment for Dad. He was a machinist—and a good one. He wanted his four boys to be engineers, so that some day all five of us would work together in a prosperous manufacturing concern of our own. Dad had ideas—patentable ideas. I, the oldest, had ideals, spoiling his project before it began.

Are idealists merely stubborn people? Whether idealistic or stubborn, I never learned to take advice. I had a mind of my own. And in that so-human vanity that characterizes all of us, I *knew* that any thought which occurred to *my* mind *had* to be ultimate truth. A strange self-awareness came over me at the age of fifteen—almost a "cosmic" awareness that I was someone special, set apart from other men. And the nightmares increased, always ending in a startled, heart-pounding wakening, halfway between a mountain top and the bottomless valley below, ever fearful that my accomplishments would not equal the ambitions.

No one shared my life. No one. On the one hand I felt too extraordinary to share my hopes; on the other hand the absence of significant fulfillment made me feel worthless. So I walked alone. There was never a close friend. It was a life born in fear and frustration.

A significant event did occur when I was twelve. We played softball and football, and I enjoyed these sports as much as the average boy. But one day I saw a basketball, and my heart began to pound. Only one who has grown up in a small town during the nineteen thirties can understand how I could have lived twelve years without seeing a basketball. I had to touch it! I had to feel that ball! For the next several days I went to the National Guard armory to watch the older boys practice basketball. The ball would bound off the court toward me. I would hesitantly move to pick it up, but always someone more aggressive got there first. One afternoon the ball fell in my hands. It was instant love. This ball was going to set me free!

"Gimme the ball!" growled a player as he snatched it from my hands. But the discovery had been made. Some men are set free by an airplane, some by the water, others by farming a piece of their own land. For me it was the basketball. At the age of twelve I tried out for the Freshman-Sophomore team.

No one can see himself as clearly as others do. So after a few days the coach (who was also our math teacher and who liked me because I did well in algebra) sidled up to me quite casually and said gently, "You know, Russell, basketball is like a lot of things. Some fellows have got it and some fellows haven't."

I pretended not to understand what he meant, but inside I was a seething mass of rage and frustration. My soul was burning with the tears I refused to release. "He will eat those words!" I vowed. And he did—the year I returned home from college with a letter in basketball. It was a road filled with ridicule and heartaches, but it was worth it, I felt. I was like a caged bird set free when I had a basketball in my hands.

I made another discovery just before my sixteenth birthday—my intelligence. Already a high school senior at fifteen, I was not yet fully aware of the mind God had given me. Until one day the mail brought a letter announcing that I had won first place in a college scholarship examination. Surely the adult world doesn't know who's coming! Surely the political world is just waiting to discover this budding young statesman!

But success in college was not simply a matter of intelligence. Intensive studying was beneath me. My grades sagged. Time that I did not spend practicing on the basketball court was idled away playing bridge and poker. Usually winning at bridge, I usually lost at poker. The trouble was, bridge was for fun and poker was for money.

God has been omitted from my story thus far. This is not entirely correct. We went to church quite regularly—every Easter. Whenever someone would invite Dad to his church, he'd file it away in the back of his mind. Sure enough, next Easter we'd show up at that church. As far as Dad was concerned, the Golden Rule was all the religion he needed to practice. He did all he could to impress honesty upon us boys. Many times I have plodded my own way through exams when I could see some of the others cheating.

A year in the Navy at the close of World War II broke into college years. The Navy almost shattered my idealism. How painful it was to discover that most people are not interested in truth: they simply want their own way. Those brief twelve months in the Navy almost brought disaster too. Like so many of the youth today, I had nothing less than contempt for constituted authority. Everyone in authority appeared ignorant, self-seeking and concerned only with maintaining the status quo. Because of this attitude I narrowly escaped a "bad-conduct" discharge. Only in retrospect can I see how many times I have been protected by a God with whom I was not on speaking terms.

I knew that God existed. I suppose that I

always accepted His reality. Did I not have a certainty in my heart that my plans were also His plans? I laid down rules for this human-divine game: "God, you stay in your heaven and don't bother me, and I'll stay here on earth and won't bother you!"

II. *Ever-closing Doors*

A college diploma with a major in history. Inevitably, so they say, the unmotivated or aimless student winds up with a B.A., majoring in history. On the basis of my own experience this could well be true. However, a political future was what I had long ago envisioned, and this normally meant a beginning career in law.

I visited a nearby large university, intending to enroll in law school. But when I looked over the curriculum and realized the necessity of speaking before crowds of people, I literally began to tremble. Why this had not occurred to me before, I do not know. The thought of speaking terrified me, for I was a totally self-centered person. I was quite uncomfortable being the center of attention. Except on the basketball court. With a basketball in my hand I was free.

Yet one night even that was ruined for me. I was playing for an independent team, and we had made it to the tournament. The games were being played on a neutral floor. Playing against a much taller team, I scored the first eight times I shot the ball—the only time this ever happened in my career. Difficult shots. Driving shots. Set shots.

Hook shots. Everything. As the sixteenth point dropped through the net, the "neutral" audience broke out in spontaneous applause. I realized that this applause was for me. Suddenly the attention had focused on me, and I couldn't bear it. I lost my freedom. The last three-quarters of that game was a nightmare. Thinking I was a superman, I began to shoot every time I got the ball. Most shots completely missed the basket. I scored only once more.

Sitting there, leafing through the law school catalog, I was filled with apprehension. Perhaps some day, but not yet. I simply could not speak in public. The totally self-centered young man.

I investigated the School of Government and discovered the field of public administration. It looked easy. And it was. I was bored. Never in my life had I been so bored during any course of study. But I was studying under the G.I. Bill and didn't dare change fields since all my school expenses were being paid by a nation caught up in a wave of patriotic gratitude. So I earned an M.A. in Government.

I decided I would rather work where there was more room for creativity and ambition, so I began to apply for jobs in private industry. This was 1949, a period of economic recession, and nobody was hiring. From company to company I traveled. I saw several personnel managers become quite enthusiastic about my educational background, but

18

their hands were tied. I began to feel the sensation of ever-closing doors.

Finally I was given an opportunity with a large grocery chain which was inaugurating a new managerial training program. After methodically working in every area of the business, I was then supposed to be equipped to be a supermarket manager. For a few months I was sent from store to store as a vacation relief manager.

I observed that the managers who got ahead were usually those who won top awards in the annual store contests. This I resolved to do when I would receive my own store. During one of the vacation relief stints I realized that I was in a "sleeper." Here was a store that could win next year's contest quite handily. I began to hope for that store.

Several weeks later the personnel manager called me in and announced that this was the very store I would receive. I could hardly wait from Friday until Monday. It was too good to be true. I was on my way up!

On Saturday night another manager almost killed himself in an automobile accident. The company needed a man to replace him immediately. I got the emergency call. It was a store very nearly without potential. The next trainee in line received the store intended for me; he won the contest and up the ladder he moved. All I saw was another closed door. I continued in the grocery business for perhaps another year of sheer frustration. My disgust carried over into my work, and at last I resigned from the company, thoroughly beaten.

I went to work for the Norfolk & Western Railway, on what turned out to be the one job I really liked. But declining business brought layoffs until I could see that I was next to be laid off. So I found another job. As I returned to pick up my final railroad pay check, the general yardmaster called me in his office. With a puzzled look on his face he asked solemnly, "Why did you quit? I was ready to begin training you for yardmaster."

Now he tells me! By this time I hated the whole world. I blamed other people, I blamed bad luck, I even blamed God in a distant sort of way. I was woefully immature. Bitterness begets bitterness, and others reacted to me in the same way I treated them. However, it seemed clear to me that everybody was against me. Periods of mild depression had always been part of my life. They began to lengthen and deepen. I scarcely knew times when there wasn't anxiety and turmoil within my heart. I was a failure—a failure as a businessman, as a husband and as a father.

Frustration and bitterness at last brought a decision of desperation. I would go to law school. This time I would do it, even with a wife and baby. I didn't know how I would be able to speak publicly, but I *would* do it. So I began to resurrect my plans to study law.

During these years one pleasant change took place in my life: we began going to church—the Church of the Brethren. To my surprise I liked the pastor. A real good guy! This was my kind of church; I loved it and supported it faithfully. For we had a church basketball team. During that six-year period we won many church league championships. That church has many dozens of trophies and is widely-known for athletic excellence if not for spiritual excellence.

This was a social bright light amid the frustrating procession of closed doors. Looking back on those years, I can almost hear the Lord wondering aloud, "How stubborn can any man be before he gets the message?"

III. *"Yes!"*

My plans were maturing. I passed the Law School Admissions Test with flying colors, as usual. Deliberately ignoring my past record on timed tests, I attempted to delude myself into believing that the high score demonstrated that I was cut out to be a law student. Apparently my human efforts this time had *forced* open some closed doors, and God decided to take more direct action. It wasn't long in coming.

Early in the spring of 1955, as I was preparing to enroll in law school for the September class, a strange phenomenon occurred. One night I awoke and opened my eyes. There in the darkness above my head I saw the word "NO." It quivered as if composed of a million wiggling, brightly-colored stars, then faded away. The next night it happened again. The same week, during the daytime, I had the experience of *feeling* that word, "NO," descend over me as if someone had dropped a very light blanket over my head. It brought an uncomfortable suffocating sensation. Again and again this daytime experience came upon me, until at last I perceived that each time I would ponder my plans for law school, that odd feeling came over me.

I quickly made the natural conclusion: God is trying to force His way into my plans. He must be made to understand that my career is to proceed as I have planned it. All that He need do is stamp it "Approved."

But how was I to go about telling God to keep His hands off my life? As the inner turmoil increased I became so desperate that I did a foolish thing: I prayed. But before I prayed I had to ask myself, "How do you pray?"

Oh, I could repeat the Lord's Prayer. During prayers in church I sat with head bowed and eyes closed, thinking of yesterday's activities or tomorrow's work. Actually I was much more comfortable downstairs helping the ushers count the Sunday offering during the worship service. So I volunteered often to help with the money. But now I knew I had to pray!

I can't pray where I'll be seen! Not this self-reliant young man! What would others think of me? After all, prayer is only for those weaklings who can't figure out things for themselves. I spent several days deciding how I would go about this matter of praying. It was almost like a native of the jungle being placed in a room where he is supposed to turn on the electric light: it could take him a long time to discover that the wall switch does the job. At last I had it all planned. I would go out and sit in the car in the middle of the night, and there I would get something straight with God if it took all night.

Once the car door was closed I didn't waste His time. "God! What's going on? What do you want from me? Don't you want me to go to law school?"

Down came that gentle, suffocating feeling: "NO." I lost the initiative, so quickly had He maneuvered me onto the defensive. "Well, do you want me to do something else?" I actually named a specific career, but what it was I have forgotten. Again came that "blanket" over my head. I inquired about a third occupation and received the same response. In exasperation I seized the initiative: "Well, I guess you want me to be a minister!"

He didn't waste my time either. "YES!" filled my being. I am almost certain that the word was not audible, yet I *heard* it. It boomed within me. It was probably that still, small voice—but a voice that had been restrained, stubbornly held off, so long that it came with a rush of intensity that I can still hear and feel.

"God! You can't do this to me! I can't stand ministers! I don't want to hold old ladies' hands!"

Wasting no time He spoke again, ever so gently: "You'll be My man. You stand on your own two feet, and I'll take care of it."

And with that the confrontation was ended.

The bells of heaven must have been ringing, but I couldn't hear them. I stepped out of the car more confused, more puzzled and more irritated than before. Yet I felt also a certainty here—that for the first time in my life there was Someone I could depend on, whether or not I liked Him.

For nearly a month I struggled with my experience. At that time I knew few ministers whom I could respect. Most pastors seemed to be "novelties" within the community, "ornamentation" used only to keep the community looking respectable. In short, they were "playing church." Someone has eloquently stated what I thought then: There are three sexes—men, women and preachers. I could never bear "religious" people.

However, those brief minutes in the car were so real that I could not forget them. The intensity with which that one word poured through me demonstrated to me how long I had been resisting. During that next month God brought a number of scenes to my mind, all of which He used to show me how long He had been speaking.

When I was in the Navy two of us sailors went to Atlantic City to visit a couple of girls for the weekend. One thing we had neglected to allow for was that my date was a minister's daughter, and the girls announced that we should see them in church on Sunday morning. We were two uncomfortable sailors, so conspicuous in our white uniforms. The girls understood. They showed us how to put on the Sunday morning false-face and look respectable. But the worst was yet to come. The guest preacher was an old-time evangelist, and during his sermon he got so carried away by his subject that he unexpectedly blurted out, "How many of you want to go to heaven? Raise your hand if you want to go to heaven!"

The nerve of that guy! Why can't some preachers quit getting so personal? Why can't he talk about something pleasant—like politics, or the weather? I was deeply offended. Every-so-often for several years that scene would pop into my mind, and each time I'd get angry all over again. God had been calling in numerous other ways too. But I had deaf ears.

Finally, after three or four weeks I surrendered: "Okay, God! I'll do it! I'll go to seminary! But you'll have to see me through!"

Suddenly I was totally aware that He *would* see me through. I simply *knew* it.

So I told my wife that I was going to be a minister. Then *she* got hysterical. If my feeling about God's call could be called resistance, there is no word to express adequately what utter loathing Norma held for the whole idea. "But why? Why do you want to be a minister?" Again and again she pleaded.

How could I explain to her that I did not want to be a minister, while all the time I was saying that we would be going to seminary? I couldn't tell her what had happened in the car. I was too ashamed to admit to anyone that I had prayed. And that my prayer was answered, and that we had carried on a conversation in the car! I knew this would give Norma all the evidence she would need to have me committed.

Norma and I met in college. She was dating a young ministerial student who roomed next to me. One evening I walked into his room and said, "Say, that's a real cute girl you're dating."

"Well, thank you, Russ."

"Yeah, I was just thinking of asking her for a date myself."

I did; and she agreed, dropping that preacher like a hot potato. Some time later, as we were making plans to be married, I asked Norma, "When I first asked you for a date, why did you drop him so quickly?"

The answer was instantaneous: "Because he's a minister, and I am not going to be a minister's wife!"

My reply was just as forceful: "Don't worry about it, honey. You won't be!"

Here I was, eight years later, welshing on my half of the bargain. No wonder Norma was hysterical! After quite a bit of emotional discussion (in which I felt I could never be completely candid), we agreed to wait a year-and-a-half. Then if this "minister-bit" still seemed to be what I should do, we would go to seminary. In this manner we each felt secretly that we might squirm out of the trap. For my part, there was the thought that perhaps God would go away and forget me.

But down deep I knew He wouldn't. And He didn't. In many little ways God showed me that my next step was seminary. If the reader has read Adela Rogers St. Johns' book, *Tell No Man*,* he knows what Norma and I felt. For I had truly told no man, not even my wife, what had happened in the car that night. I was too ashamed of the ridicu-

* Doubleday, 1966.

lousness of the whole experience. I could not bear being the butt of scornful laughter. Yet the event was so real that I had to deal with it.

At last, writing off all my hopes and swallowing my pride—literally, I had to eat my self-respect —I prepared to leave for seminary. For I knew that if I refused to go, God would close doors in my face the rest of my stubborn life. I was enrolling in seminary, strangely enough, without any recollection of having heard even once a single presentation of the Gospel of Jesus Christ.

A few days before we were to leave, a friend in the congregation which licensed me to the ministry stepped up and said, "Russ, I know it's going to cost money. If I can help in any way, let me know." Later he spoke again, more urgently: "Just let me know how much you need. I mean it. Don't hesitate to call on me."

God's providential timing! We were to need that financial help almost as soon as we arrived.

Seventeen months and several heated arguments after He called, we left Virginia for Bethany Biblical Seminary, the Church of the Brethren seminary then located in Chicago. Obediently Norma came along, but we both felt terribly unclean and hypocritical.

IV. *The New Creation*

An interested student, but a confused preacher!
If studies could make a minister, it would have
been simple. It is one thing to know the New Testament, another to know the One about whom the
New Testament was written. Unfortunately I
brought all my old frustrations and hostilities with
me to seminary. Many of my classmates and professors still think of me as the moody personality
which could easily erupt in irritation. I didn't
know why I was in seminary, and yet I did know.

The tension grew as the first year progressed.
For ministers must speak in public perhaps as
much as lawyers. Seminary students are ordinarily
required to accept summer pastorates in small congregations or in larger churches temporarily without pastors. I repeatedly told myself, "Russ, one
of these days you've got to stand in a pulpit and
tell several hundred people about God." And I
cried out in lonely despair, "But I don't know
Him! How can I tell others publicly?"

We were expecting our second child in August,
so I was exempted from a summer pastorate—for
that year. Since Norma would hardly have agreed
to a new baby each summer, sooner or later I would

have to preach. I was a pathetic figure, standing alone in the practice preaching pulpit, with sympathetic professors and students trying to help me. How I thank God for those patient, patient professors! But I was so turned in on myself that they could hardly get through the barriers I had erected.

Norma's attitude was, as it had been, negative; but God told her at some point in her struggles that she should be obedient and accompany me to seminary. And she *was* trying to cooperate, but it was drudgery for her. So we had our problems that year. Financial problems too. Although I had once been assured that God would see us through, when the time came to claim delivery on that promise, I was absolutely devoid of faith. Yet the money came. Many times we were without a single penny, and money would come from the most unexpected sources.

The first Christmas looked bleak indeed. We wondered how we would eat. It was the low point financially of the three years—a prolonged drought of income. With absolutely no faith in the God who had directed me there, I worried myself into depression again. Bills were piling up. We ate our meals, but that was all. The friend who so graciously loaned us money to begin seminary had to explain painfully how his resources were now limited by another matter, and he was sorry. Shortly on the heels of his letter came a letter from someone else, containing a check for two hundred dollars! A small amount today perhaps, but to us it was like ten thousand dollars. We hadn't a penny in the house.

A local pastor asked several of us seminary students to help him in the rehabilitation of an ex-convict. This pastor commented one day that he was afraid that the ex-convict did "not have a personal relationship with Jesus Christ." The statement hit me like a shotgun blast. A rush of conflicting thoughts assaulted my brain. "I never heard such a statement before! What is this guy— a fundamentalist (whatever that was)? Does this pastor think he's better than I am? No, that ex-convict doesn't have a personal relationship with Jesus Christ, and neither do I. I should ask him about it. No, don't ask; he'll just embarrass you. Look, you're supposed to be a ministerial student— don't admit you haven't got it. What am I doing here in seminary, anyway? I'm just a big hypocrite!" And I shoved this one too—down into that already-chaotic emptiness.

By the end of the year numerous bills were piling up, and there was no summer employment in sight. At the last minute a good-paying job opened up, as well as an additional part time job. The money rolled in all summer, and the final week's paycheck paid the last of the long-standing bills.

The second seminary year began, and that ominous feeling slowly returned. Next summer, Russ. Next summer you've *got* to preach. The anxiety increased.

The schedule irritated me too. We were required to take a course called "Devotional Life"

—or its equivalent. I wasn't able to work out an equivalent, so I resigned myself to the ordeal. The course was not what disturbed me. It was the professor—a ridiculous little old lady who cackled when she laughed—Dr. Anna Mow, affectionately known across the whole world as "Sister Anna."

We had a large class, and she could hardly give us individual attention; yet I began to feel as if I were receiving individual attention. Sister Anna spoke of Jesus as if she knew Him. Some of us would leave class shaking our heads at her strange personality; yet within a few weeks my laughter ended, my curiosity was aroused, and before Christmas I was hungrily devouring every word she spoke and every devotional reading she recommended. The Bible began to read differently, especially the New Testament. I felt myself beginning to pray spontaneously (I was still afraid of intimate prayer—ever since the experience in the car). But now my fears of God, my resentments against Him, began to melt. I could feel *love*— trickling, then flowing, and finally gushing into my softened heart. The world looked different. I began to smile more. Sister Anna had given me a personal introduction to the second Person of the Trinity. This time I *heard* heaven's bells ringing!

Over the Christmas holidays I had a warehouse job, on which I was all alone. Every spare minute I spent devouring the New Testament. One day I came to John 3:3, where Jesus told Nicodemus, "Unless one is born anew, he cannot see the kingdom of God."

"That's me!" I shouted, jumping straight up from the chair. "That's me! I've been born anew!"

I leaped around that room, laughing hilariously and crying profusely. That lonely warehouse job was God's Christmas gift to me. I knew Him! I knew Him! Excitedly I turned to various scriptures that had previously been clouded from my perception. Every one of them made sense. Every one. "God! I know you! Jesus! I know you!"

I have heard lots of profound and not-so-profound arguments in the twelve years since, but there is no argument that can shake an actual experience. Soon I discovered another precious verse, 2 Corinthians 5:17: "Therefore, if any one is in Christ, he is a new creation; the old has passed away, behold, the new has come." The thrill of the new birth was inexpressible. Now I knew the meaning of salvation. Now I too had a personal relationship with Jesus Christ. Now I knew that my place in heaven was assured. Prayer became as natural as breathing.

Suddenly I wanted to tell people about Jesus Christ. Oh, how I wish summer were here, so I could preach about Him! My! I *must* be a new creation! I can hardly wait to get into a pulpit! Now I knew what I had wished for so long: one need not be religious to be a Christian. Jesus' own problems were almost exclusively with religious people.

Herein too lay frustrations. The other students weren't interested in my experience. Most of them had hearts as hard as mine had been. But, I discovered, for a different reason. Nearly all of them had grown up attending church every Sunday. They had been *inoculated* against the new birth! In little doses they had built up a massive resistance to the real faith. Norma too. Always close to the church, she could see by my personality, my warmth and my new interest in life that something good had happened to me, but she was afraid to talk to me about it. Her resentment against God had yet to be dispelled. So I would sit in class or lie in bed, quietly giggling to myself, enjoying something I don't think God ever intended—a solitary conversion.

The summer pastorate must be recorded as the first pleasant experience of any duration that I ever had. The sensation of deep satisfaction with life was a new source of exhilaration. How wonderful life can be when I no longer live for myself alone! How wonderful to know that the Almighty Creator of the whole universe stands behind me! And I preached with conviction.

The tears flowed freely that last Sunday of August. Truly, there can never be another congregation so wonderful as these lovely people. I told myself that in all the pastorates I will hold after I graduate, this one will cling to my heart as unique in the Church of the Brethren. We returned for my senior year with mixed joy and sadness.

V. *Pittsburgh*

Knowing Jesus Christ on a personal basis made seminary life different. The Bible enabled me to discern truth and falsehood, or perhaps the distinction should be made between God's truth and man's opinions. A seminary curriculum is full of both, especially the latter. The constant bombardment with statements of unbelief and human conjecture took its toll. During my senior year the joy leveled off, then began to dissipate slowly but surely.

Studying however came easier. My grades went up. I wasn't too surprised on Commencement Day to hear the words *cum laude* following the reading of my name. How I wanted to tell everyone Who was responsible! But few were interested. I was trying to keep alive my relationship with my Lord, but without the like-minded fellowship of other believers I was having a struggle.

As we began to look forward to a full-time pastorate, Norma and I discussed where we'd like to go. To our mutual surprise we agreed that we would like a rural or small-town church—most certainly away from the city. I envisioned an older building, small, with a pleasant warmth that makes a newcomer feel welcome immediately, and a small congregation of friendly folks with genuine Christian hospitality. A country church.

One March evening the telephone rang, and the speaker on the other end identified himself as Chairman of the Ministerial Commission of the Pittsburgh Church of the Brethren. "Would you like to come and preach a trial sermon for us?"

My mind was set with the answer: "No, I would not like to come and preach a trial sermon." But I heard a soft voice which seemed to come from right behind my head, a voice which awakened a four-year-old memory. He spoke gently while I hesitated: "There it is, Russ; go to it!" God has never used King James language in speaking to me. He speaks in such a way that I can't miss the point. And He has taught me to communicate with Him in the same manner.

Reluctantly I agreed to come to Pittsburgh to meet with the congregation. On Sunday morning I stood up to preach a trial sermon. The congregation had been having difficulties finding a pastor. It seemed that nobody wanted to come. So they were as tense and nervous as I was. I gave a few words of greeting, then leaned heavily on the pulpit. The top of the lectern tipped forward, and my weight fell on it with a resounding bang! Someone had lifted the top to examine it and had neglected to replace it in the proper locking position. I caught the lectern quickly, or it would have gone crashing to the floor. The congregation tightened perceptibly. "There goes *another* pastor! He'll be so embarrassed he would never come here!'' I replaced the lectern and looked up at the congregation. I felt the strongest urge to smile. And when the smile came, a spontaneous wisecrack followed, and I continued with the sermon. Norma commented later that I could have sat down at that moment, and they would have voted a unanimous call.

They did—that evening. We agreed that I should begin my pastorate in Pittsburgh the following September. On the plane, returning to seminary, I pondered the uncharacteristic poise I had displayed in that pulpit. My sober face only occasionally would break into a smile. I hadn't yet learned to perceive Who really inspired that grin.

We arrived at the Pittsburgh Church of the Brethren September 2, 1959, at two a.m., to find three of the members waiting there for us. They helped us unload, tucked us in bed and went home. Next morning we opened the refrigerator to find everything we needed for a delicious breakfast, as well as sufficient food for many additional meals.

After breakfast I walked next door to the church building. It's an older building, small, with a pleasant warmth that makes a newcomer feel welcome immediately. Soon I discovered that it was a small congregation of friendly folks filled with genuine Christian hospitality. What do you know, I thought—a country church right in the middle of the city! Thinking I was giving up my desires in order to obey God's wishes, He wonderfully honored my obedience by granting my desires also.

We felt so welcome! The parsonage had been

newly painted. Wall-to-wall carpet and draperies had been installed. Old fixtures had been replaced by new. Perhaps it looked old on the outside, but inside it was attractive and comfortable.

My interests lay with the congregation. Did they know Jesus Christ? How were they serving Him? This proved to be somewhat of a disappointment, for the Gospel was rather a foreign proclamation to many. Within a short time I had been offered several committee positions at the Church of the Brethren District level. Most of our pastors are involved in such jobs. I turned them down to devote all my time to the spiritual nurture of this congregation. The Church had been without a pastor for more than a year, and various laymen were fulfilling all sorts of responsibilities. Several said, "Am I glad you're here at last so I can get rid of this responsibility!"

In most cases I answered, "You've been doing such a good job and I'm so new, would you mind continuing for a while?" They just couldn't turn me down. The laymen are still doing those jobs— and enjoying them. My responsibilities, as I saw them, were largely spiritual. God had outlined my part of the work before I came, and I intended to stick with His outline.

Interest soared. Attendance rose sharply. The offerings increased steadily. Everyone was so attentive while I preached. So many would comment favorably on my sermons following the service. One couple even told me that they hesitated to go away for a weekend for fear that they would "miss something." My messages were being received, I thought. And I began to tell myself, "Russ, you're a pretty good preacher."

One Sunday, about six months after we arrived in Pittsburgh, I was preaching my usual superb sermon when my attention was distracted by a woman's elbow, making a quick jab into her husband's ribs. His head jerked up, his eyes blinked and he sat there stiffly. Soon my eye was caught by her elbow, once again sharply pushed into his side. And again his head shot up and his eyes opened. "This guy is going to sleep during *my sermon!*" I thought. "What's wrong with him? Doesn't he realize that I have something important to say to him? Doesn't he know that he can profit by this sermon if he'll just listen?"

It was no use. His wife gave up, and I "gave him up." He slept through the remainder of the sermon. The organ music woke him. As he went out the door he had the brightest, most refreshed smile on his face. And he said, "Russ, that was a wonderful sermon!"

Every new pastor ought to have such an experience. God chose such a means to cause me to take a second look at myself. Was anything *really* happening in the Church? Yes, according to this world's standards. But how many were accepting Jesus Christ and discovering Him personally, as I had just a couple years before? I had to admit that little of real importance was occurring.

This realization should have put me on my

knees more often, but it didn't. I needed the fellowship and mutual inspiration of other like-minded ministers to push me into growing in Christ. I was lonely. While I had learned to appreciate the faith of the fundamentalists and their respect for the authority of scripture, most of them seemed lacking in the outward manifestations of what was inside them—the love and the good works. They were argumentative; their doctrines were closed, with no room for growth. I needed fellowship that would inspire me to grow. Nearly all my friends in the ministry were liberals. Intellectually we got along fine, but when we began discussing Jesus Christ they would act as if I had leprosy. So I was lonely.

Many ministers can be quite content to maintain the status quo, live a good life, raise a family and be little concerned about concrete results. But God didn't construct me that way. The lack of results pushed me into beginning a course of study leading to a master's degree at nearby Pittsburgh Theological Seminary. How many frustrated pastors are walking that same path every day, retreating into an academic world!

Only a few weeks of classes were needed to show me that my own efforts had misfired again. Norma, always my best sermon critic, who I knew would never be merely flattering, commented one day, ''Your sermons are still good, but since you began school, you've gotten so *intellectual.*''

I resisted what she was saying—indeed, what God was saying. But not for long. The graduate study was dropped abruptly. Since then I have taken many varied, non-credit courses as I felt the need, including six highly-profitable semesters of

Hebrew and Greek, which I had not studied during my seminary years.

When I had once again seen the folly of my own way, God moved in with His way. A neighboring pastor asked me one day if I would care to attend a weekly breakfast prayer meeting with a few other pastors, including the pastor of Calvary Episcopal Church, Dr. Sam Shoemaker. I leaped at the opportunity.

VI. *Glimpses Through the Door*

My homiletics professor had said during the last months of seminary, "Russ, you're very fortunate to be going to Pittsburgh. That's where Sam Shoemaker is." One of Shoemaker's books had been required reading in our homiletics class. That book had made a deep impression on me.

"Dr. Sam" had also hit Pittsburgh with an impact. Already instrumental in founding Alcoholics Anonymous, Faith at Work, Young Life and The Fellowship of Christian Athletes, Sam was in Pittsburgh only a short time when he began to challenge the young, social-climbing, junior-executive types to give their lives to Christ. Out of this grew the Pittsburgh Experiment, an interdenominational group which has sponsored effective prayer groups all over the area. Many business, professional and blue collar workers participate. The Pittsburgh Experiment has proved to discerning business and political leaders that a committed Christian makes a better employee and a better citizen.

Sam Shoemaker had something I wanted. I was going to get it.

A number of young ministers, attracted by the

prominent name, began to attend our breakfast meetings. But when they discovered that Sam was always pushing for a radical transformation of life, many of them dropped out after two or three meetings. Sam was either a joy or a disappointment; few could remain neutral around him.

At the prayer breakfasts I observed that Sam was continually referring to "the Holy Spirit," and in a most personal sense. Slowly I too began to sense the reality and presence of God's Holy Spirit. Some of the old joy returned as here in our prayer breakfasts came a taste of the fellowship I craved. My preaching changed perceptibly. Discovering that the Holy Spirit honors with His presence the faithful preaching of God's word, I began to notice the improvement on the tape recorder. The words of my sermons were the same, but they came out differently. The extreme "flatness" of my voice was noticeably moderated. Quietly, subtly, the Holy Spirit performed His work so that I could not discern it except by comparing a current tape with a sermon from six months before.

I was growing. And slowly little changes could be perceived in the congregation. Occasionally there would appear in the pews a brightened countenance which I hadn't noticed before. Someone had entered the kingdom of God. Asking eagerly how they happened to receive the new birth (thinking, of course, "I wonder which one of my sermons did it?"), one would reply hesitantly, "Oh, it happened over at so-and-so's house, in his prayer meeting." Or perhaps the answer would be, "I gave my life to Christ at a Billy Graham Crusade."

How deflating! Nothing seemed to happen while I was preaching. Yet God has been trying to show me over many years that I can do nothing unless *He* does it—through me. He began to reveal to me that my faithful Sunday-after-Sunday proclamation of His word was essential, that although I wasn't reaping the harvest, I was planting good seed. That was encouraging.

One day another Church of the Brethren pastor called. In recent weeks he had been profoundly affected by a Faith at Work Conference and by Sam Shoemaker. Would I like to organize a regular prayer group among some of the Brethren pastors of the greater Pittsburgh area? I wondered if this could be for real. Our denomination seemed so spiritually dead. Four of us Church of the Brethren ministers began to meet each Tuesday for lunch, and we witnessed the Holy Spirit doing many precious works within us and within our congregations. Defeat and despair appear so often among sincere pastors, and in that Tuesday prayer group we learned to confide in each other, support and pray for one another. Every one of us rode through some difficult storms unscathed and often emerged stronger and more mature.

With only brief respites my life had been an intense, lonely struggle all the way. Little-by-little I began to perceive "the body of Christ" in these other pastors. "No man is an island." That included me. We needed each other, and I discovered that the Holy Spirit would deal lovingly with my needs as I would permit some life-long, fear-bred barriers to crumble. The risk of exposing oneself in a Christ-centered group is not really much of a gamble.

Through these years God led me into a greater trust in the authenticity of the scriptures. This had to be *faith*, growing in me. My questioning mind had always demanded verification. When I graduated from seminary I was teetering on this issue of the authenticity of scripture. I believed all the major doctrines of Christianity. The intellectual assaults on the virgin birth also assaulted me. Because God had performed a miracle in my heart, I knew that if He had wanted His Son born in such a manner, He could have done it. Yet the furor over the virgin birth seemed to me all out of proportion to its doctrinal importance, so I tended to avoid any comment on it because of the emotions it would stir up. How much more vital, it has always appeared to me, are the crucifixion and the resurrection!

But I was sidestepping a much larger issue. Do I believe the scriptures to be true, or do I reserve for myself the privilege of treating the Bible like a cafeteria—accepting what I want and ignoring the rest? The Church of the Brethren has always been known as a New Testament Church. Traditionally we have looked upon the Old Testament as authentic only as perceived through the window of the New. This principle could be stated similarly, The Bible is God's progressive self-revelation.

My approach to scripture bothered me for several years after seminary, for the Holy Spirit had been urging me to take a leap of faith. My inherent honesty caused me to hold Him off for a time. After all, had I not seen the three-storied universe demythologized? Didn't I see clearly that the "demons" or "evil spirits" of the New Testament were nothing more than personality maladjustments or merely the symptoms of actual physical illnesses?

A lot of prayer, Bible-study and heart-searching went into a difficult ultimate decision: "Yes, Lord, I believe the Bible is true. On faith I say to you that I no longer reserve for myself the privilege of accepting or rejecting particular portions. I accept it all as truth." This act, I can now see in retrospect, has proven to be one of the most critical and vital conscious decisions of my entire life.

Many Christians, in their precious simplicity, have little idea of the struggles of the intellectual. Points which seem trivial to the average Christian will cause violent reactions within the mind of a true intellectual. My turmoil lasted several years on this issue alone. The lifelong search for truth finally culminated in the Bible, and Jesus Christ in particular.

From that time I could begin to tell the congregation—and I did so in many ways—"Do not trust your traditions, nor your opinions, nor your feelings, nor the way you were taught. Trust the Bible, especially the New Testament." This continues to be a favorite theme.

Within several more years I would be taking a huge dose of my own medicine.

Sam Shoemaker had given me a nodding acquaintance with the third Person of the Trinity. I grew—some. But Sam, by his own confession, never stepped far inside the door. He peered in, liked what he saw, but hesitated to step boldly into the "walk in the Spirit." So he stayed near the door in order, he felt, to show others the handle.

But I too had experienced a few glimpses through that door.

VII. *Twila's Call*

When a man comes to Christ, he brings with him a lot of excess baggage. I brought a truckload. One bit of unwanted baggage was my skepticism of the supernatural. I recall Dad, when this issue of someone's alleged supernatural power came up, asked me bluntly, "Did it happen to you?"

I admitted that it hadn't. "Then don't believe it!" That was my teenage indoctrination in the miraculous. I learned to believe only what I could see and touch. My education served only to deepen my skepticism.

So when I graduated from seminary I gave the Lord another ultimatum: "I want to serve you in whatever way I can, but don't expect me to believe this divine healing stuff." Thus I constructed merely one more fence which the Holy Spirit would have to kick down. For He had called me to be a minister in the Church of the Brethren, a New Testament denomination with a 250-year history of practicing the anointing of the sick.

The Lord wasn't tardy in dealing with me on this issue. Within five months after I arrived in Pittsburgh a crisis came. The telephone rang. It was Twila: "Reverend Bixler, would you please come and anoint my husband?"

I squirmed. "Well-uh-are you sure he's that sick?"

"He's had a heart attack!"

"Well-uh-let's see—how about later in the week?"

"Reverend Bixler, I'd like it today."

There was no way out. I staggered through the anointing. I was so embarrassed, trying to read a service out of a book while holding both hands on the sick man's head, an effort that normally requires three hands. As always, I was quite uncomfortable taking part in something which I didn't believe. A feeling of being dirty, hypocritical, swept over me. When I had finished I just wanted to go home and take a bath.

The heart attack victim? He appeared to experience no more than the normal recovery.

For the next anointing I asked one of our older deacons to assist. Again I prayed my embarrassed prayer, then listened as the deacon prayed. Slowly the awareness grew that "This guy actually believes that healing jazz!" I was astonished! "And I asked him because I thought he was a level-headed man!"

This time the patient improved much more rapidly than expected, in spite of my unbelief. Soon I learned that we had two deacons who believed strongly that God heals through the anointing; thereafter when called for an anointing I would depend upon their faith. And we saw God perform a few delightful things—"little" miracles, they might be called. Of course, each time the patient improved the thought would come into my mind, "Isn't it amazing what the power of suggestion will do?" *That* voice I hadn't yet learned to identify.

But I was wavering. I had always believed what I could see and touch, and there was slowly accumulating ample evidence to be seen and touched.

One day Eleanor called. She had been suffering from severe back pain and had had Xrays taken. "The doctor is to tell me the results of the Xrays, and I don't have a ride. Would you take me?"

So we drove to see the doctor. After a few minutes in his office, Eleanor walked out with the doctor. His manner was quite sober. Her expression was one of shock. He had announced gravely that her lower spine was full of arthritis. Eleanor naively asked, "Well, what can be done about it?" He was forced to tell her that while its spread could be checked, nothing could be done to eliminate the arthritic condition that already existed. Of course, there were medicines to alleviate the pain.

The very thought of a lifetime of such pain could drive people to suicide. Eleanor was 25 years old and the mother of two little boys. As we rode home in the car I was berating myself, "Here I am, her pastor, and I have nothing to offer this poor girl but sympathy!" In desperation I offered the anointing service, trying to exude a superficial confidence that all would be right, while inside that same voice went into instant action: "Now you've done it! This one is different. The arthritis is there, in black and white, on the Xrays. And didn't the doctor say it was permament? No power of suggestion will work this time. How will you squirm out of this one?"

But I had done it. I had offered Eleanor a faint glimmer of hope, all the while there was little faith within me. Like Eleanor, I knew astonishingly little about arthritis. So I did some inquiring from knowledgeable persons. My heart sank.

Then a name widely associated with the healing ministry was given to me. A friend mentioned Emily Gardiner Neal, a free-lance writer of books and magazine articles who lives in Pittsburgh. Still putting off the anointing, I wrote to Mrs. Neal, explaining Eleanor's predicament. She phoned the next day, saying in her husky voice that she was glad to have received the letter and, yes, she did know of quite a number of cases of arthritis which God had healed.

"Well, we will be anointing Eleanor tomorrow evening."

"Good! Our prayer group will be meeting, and we'll pray at the very time you anoint her."

Together a deacon and I went to her house at the appointed hour. The sight was appalling. Eleanor could no longer lie or sit comfortably. In a half-reclining position she tried gamely to greet us. If there remained even one spark of faith in my heart, it must have fled at that moment. Her pain was intense. The whole family was almost paralyzed with fear. We anointed her, prayed and left.

As we rode home in the car, I was overwhelmed by tears of rage and frustration. "Look how she's suffering, and all I can do is anoint her and pray for her!"

All I can do! Within several days God gave Eleanor a clean spine. One week later she was on her hands and knees, scrubbing the kitchen floor and praising God. Her pain had grown almost unbearable the night after she was anointed, but the next day it began to moderate until she felt normal. Subsequent Xrays revealed a spine totally healed of arthritis. The doctor said with tears in his eyes, "Eleanor, you're a miracle. You're a miracle."

I was overjoyed—and burdened. There was a decision to be made. My honesty demanded a definite decision. I had two choices—either to believe that God works healing miracles today or to close my eyes to the truth once and for all. That painful decision cost me one of my favorite opinions. That opinion was utterly demolished under the healing power of God's Holy Spirit.

I read somewhere that a group of scientists set about determining how much pain is involved when a man is forced by evidence to change his mind. It was said that such an experience carries pain equivalent to the most exquisite torture.

I believe it.

The boldness God gave me was astounding. "Eleanor, why don't we ask the Lord to heal your colitis?"

"Oh, I don't think so. I've had colitis for twelve years. I'll just have to put up with it."

"Well, we'll see. It won't hurt to ask God. Let's talk to Mrs. Neal again."

We set an appointment for Mrs. Neal's apartment. She and I laid hands on Eleanor's head and asked the Father, in Jesus' name, to heal Eleanor of the colitis. That was in March. Each week I asked Eleanor whether the colitis was still present. And each week her countenance would darken to say that she was no better. The weekly question-and-answer grew so embarrassing that I stopped asking.

One day in July, as she was eating lunch, Eleanor realized with a start that she was eating food that formerly caused great discomfort. And though she searched her memory, she could not recall how long she had been eating these foods with no ill effects. The Holy Spirit again, this time quietly and gently, healed her body.

Eleanor herself is the greatest miracle. From the pain of childhood traumas and her developing hostilities, she has been transformed by Jesus Christ into a delightful blessing to countless others. The Holy Spirit has placed her in numerous situations where her testimony has brought unbelievers to tears. Eleanor's understanding of extreme pain gives her a special ministry to other sufferers, many of whom as a result have also received God's healing touch.

To the glory of God, a sizable number in our congregation were growing right along with me.

The first instantaneous healing was quite a thrill. The wide-eyed surprise of the patient and those precious words, "It's gone! The pain is gone!" still bring tears to my eyes.

I grew bolder and soon began to preach on God's healing power. I was hoping for a way to have the entire congregation witness a healing. For many of our members had hearts as firmly closed as mine had been.

In October 1965, I was preaching for a week of meetings in another city, when a lady gave me the name and address of a young woman in the Pittsburgh area who she said was in great spiritual need. I went to see her the very next week.

Becky was hard. No other word could describe her. She was "hard as nails." To my surprise she appeared at the church on Sunday morning. A few weeks later I asked her how she was feeling, and she explained hesitantly that she had some mysterious ailment. For some reason my mind was closed to her words. I could not recall later that she had ever mentioned an illness.

But Becky was indeed a sick young woman. She is a registered nurse and knew her illness was desperate. That was why she began to show an interest in the church. As she realized the nature of her illness she turned to God. While she listened to a radio preacher one day, the music touched a hungry spot in her heart, and Becky began to cry.

From repeated childhood beatings and cursings she had steeled herself not to cry. During nurse's training she had attempted suicide. Becky was a fighter. Her whole family knew that all too well.

She had not shed a tear since childhood. But as the music flowed so did the tears. And Jesus moved into her hard heart.

One day, two months after Becky had begun to attend our church, the telephone rang. A girl was crying on the other end, and for some seconds I could not discern whose voice I heard. It was Becky. She had just returned from the doctor's office. I inquired as to what was wrong. "Don't you remember that I told you I was sick?"

I was embarrassed, but piece-by-piece the details came out. Becky had *myositis ossificans.* "What's that?" I asked.

She explained that it is a disease in which bone begins to form in the neck and shoulder areas. Normally it is a very painful chronic ailment and many victims survive for years. This day however the doctor had been quite alarmed over the rapid progress of the disease and announced that hers was an acute case. Becky went home and opened her medical books. There she noted that she had perhaps ten horrible years to face before some vital organ would fail and death would come. Already her neck and shoulders were wooden from the developing bone. The pain and muscle spasms were increasing.

While holding the telephone I knew that Becky was the one we were awaiting. I proposed an anointing service before the entire congregation, one week from the coming Sunday. She was quite reluctant and agreed only after my assurances that we would do nothing to embarrass her. Her illness was announced the first Sunday, and we asked everyone to pray during that week. The following Sunday she came to church with a smile on her face. "I've been reprieved from the death sentence. I know it! Something is beginning to happen!"

That morning I spoke on divine healing, giving some of the biblical bases for this ministry. Then we called Becky to kneel at the front while our congregational moderator and the chairman of the deacon board assisted me in anointing her. When Becky stood up the pain was gone. The hardness in her shoulders and neck disappeared slowly, over a three-week period. But she was healed instantaneously that Sunday morning and she knew it. The whole congregation had a wonderful opportunity to witness first-hand the love and the power of God. We received a double blessing that day.

True, there were a few who would have been much happier if Becky had continued to grow worse. They resented her healing. Many church members have a faith which gives no room to a Jesus Christ who is the same yesterday and today and for ever. They are quite comfortable with a distant God who hasn't done anything significant in 2,000 years. Such a public demonstration of His very present power would obviously threaten to shatter their illusions.

Ever-so-gently the Holy Spirit has been softening Becky's scarred personality. Today she is the strongest "prayer warrior" in the congregation, with a powerful ministry of intercessory prayer. Such healings as Becky's were rare. Perhaps once each year-or-two we would see the Holy Spirit pour out His power so dramatically. However, the overall health of the congregation was improving noticeably.

A neighboring pastor called, asking me to assist him in anointing a woman in his congregation. She was suffering from *tic douloureux,* which I once heard described as the most excruciating physical pain known to man. When we arrived and listened to her story, I could believe what I had heard. She had been spending each night in the basement, where her screams would not be heard by the rest of the family. We anointed her and left. That night her suffering was the worst she had experienced, but with the daylight she was completely healed by a loving God in response to the simple anointing and prayer of His servants.

There were still occasional premature deaths in our congregation. Each one hit me a harder blow. I stood outside the oxygen tent of a mother who was sorely needed at home and cursed the illness that was taking her life. I vowed at that moment of intense rage an undying war upon the curses of pain, disease and death—until Jesus Christ finally destroys that last enemy.

I have never been able to accept suffering, either in myself or in others. I am absolutely of no use if sympathy is needed or if a comforting touch would be helpful. My bedside manner is one of impatience. My only intention in dealing with the sick is seeing what can be done about a complete cure. And I was discovering in the Holy Spirit a personal Power who wanted the same. He was the Power and He was teaching me to depend upon Him.

One spring we received a letter from the wife of a Church of the Brethren doctor, a medical missionary in the mountains of Puerto Rico. Mrs. Smith stated that their son David, who was thirteen years old, had been born with an open spine, paralyzed from the waist down. For ten years he had remained approximately the same, until his parents came to the decision that it was *not* God's will that David should be handicapped in any way. From the time they began to pray for his healing, there had been very slow but noticeable improvement. The Smiths would be returning to the States in July. They were asking if they could stay at our house while they took David to a Kathryn Kuhlman Miracle Service.

Really! we thought. A doctor who would go to a Kathryn Kuhlman service! On the radio Miss Kuhlman sounded too raucous for us, so we had always avoided her ministry. But now, as good hosts, Norma and I should attend the service with the Smiths.

David was a precious boy. He had committed his life to Jesus Christ, and his greatest ambition was to have the Lord heal him. We wheeled him into the service that Friday morning and sat down to witness a stream of miracles, many as dramatic as what we had been seeing only once each year. I watched; I studied everything closely; and I prayed that God would reveal some of His truth to me in that service. Most of all, every one of us was praying for David.

We saw no outward improvement in David, but his father received instantaneous healing for a sinus condition. Dr. Smith gave a thrilling personal testimony at the microphone. And the Holy Spirit taught me. I prayed, "Lord, let the same things happen in our Church—without the 'showy' atmosphere, if you please."

From that very day the Pittsburgh Church of the Brethren continued for two-and-a-half years without a death!

VIII. *A Tragedy Opens the Door*

A week of camp counseling was a pleasant but exhausting annual experience which I endured for several years. A number of the teenagers sensed that I had a message for them, some answers they were seeking; but few came for help. I lacked the "power" to draw them. They liked my guitar however.

When I was twelve years old Dad had decided that I should play the guitar and he paid his hard-earned money for lessons. A year-and-a-half the lessons continued—until his dream and my nightmare finally were dispelled by the realization that I simply didn't have what was required. But I remembered the chords and could begin to play folk music with the teenagers who had guitars at camp.

We saw the movie, "Mary Poppins," and the song, "Feed the Birds," captured my heart. "That melody is too beautiful to be wasted on secular words," I decided. I knew God was going to give me His words for that lovely song. During recreation period at youth camp that summer, I sat for an hour in the cabin, praying and writing. At the end of the hour the words were written, and we all sang "Pilgrim's Hymn" next day. The Holy Spirit had used me in a new way!

Seven years I had been pastor of this congregation. For all the good things God was doing, I was still impatient. Our Church should be, as someone has said, "a hospital for sinners, not a rest home for saints." Many of the members hadn't moved an inch with the Lord in all those years. Some of them very humanly reasoned, "These things are not God's doing; they are Russ Bixler's doing." I was comforted by the fact that Jesus had had the same accusation thrown at him. It was so clear to me that our congregation should be doing more, much more.

Occasionally through the years we would hear about some Brethren from out-of-town who had a family member in one of our Pittsburgh hospitals. We would invite the one accompanying the sick person to spend his nights in our guest room. Then I began to wonder, "If I know of this many who need housing, how many more must there be who come and go and we never hear of them?" The Holy Spirit organized a plan in my heart: Offer the congregation's spare bedrooms to members of the Church of the Brethren from the areas which would feed into the Pittsburgh hospitals. As so many have said, Love is something you do!

The idea was proposed to the deacon board and was seriously discussed there. Those who had no extra bedroom felt uneasy, but we agreed to try it. We took a map and drew a line separating us from the Cleveland—Philadelphia—Baltimore—Washington—Charlottesville—Columbus areas. Then we prepared a letter to send to each Church of the

Brethren within that irregular circle. There were more than two hundred churches! With some trepidation we sent the following letter:

December 1966

Dear Brethren:

We, the members of the Pittsburgh Church of the Brethren, would like to offer our assistance to our fellow-members of the Church of the Brethren.

Realizing that there are many highly-specialized medical doctors in our city, and that the Brethren are occasionally required by serious illness or accident to be hospitalized in Pittsburgh, we welcome any accompanying family members to be guests in our homes during this period.

We realize also that hospitalization can be an expensive matter, especially when it must take place some distance from home. We offer beds, meals, our concern and our prayers. Our ministers and deacons are available at any time for visiting and for the anointing for healing.

Such circumstances can be a period of great tension, even tragedy; so we want you to feel at home in our homes. In the event of critical illness, we can accommodate any close relatives who feel obligated to come.

Please be assured of our full commitment to this service. We are deeply convinced that our Lord has blessed us in many ways, including spare bedrooms; so we wish in this manner to do what we can for Him. We want no financial compensation. Our only regret is that we are offering ourselves many years too late.

If you can, phone or write before you leave home. *Please* do not hesitate to call upon us. Contact . . .

In His service,
The Pittsburgh Church

With one exception we have always been able to find accommodations easily. We have never had

65

to turn down any of the Brethren. Surprisingly there have been extended periods with no requests for our hospitality. Thus we named it—our "Hospitality Project." The results have been good. We had scarcely realized the terrible loneliness and fear which can strike one of the small-town or rural Brethren, stranded alone in Pittsburgh with a husband or wife in critical condition. After a couple years' experience the Western Pennsylvania District Executive Secretary requested my evaluation of the Hospitality Project for the district newsletter. This is the article that was printed.

First, they [the Pittsburgh congregation] have a firm conviction that God has placed this ministry upon them, and that they are fulfilling His divine command through this particular congregation in this particular location.

Second, the project has drawn the congregation closer to the rest of the Brotherhood. There are few Brethren living in the Pittsburgh area, which has sometimes made them feel isolated. Each family involved in the project has established close ties of friendship and love with other Brethren families from out-of-town.

Third, they have noted a problem in that none of their members live near the hospitals and the folks who stay with them usually need to drive their own cars or take the transit system back and forth each day. It's a new experience for rural Brethren in the big city.

Fourth, they have seen the healing ministry tremendously broadened. Names of the sick Brethren are printed in the Sunday bulletin, and the congregation prays for them, thus agreeing in prayer with their home congregations (Matthew 18:19). Mrs. Harold Wolfe, project chairman, and others visit whenever possible. They have discovered that many Brethren are open to any miracle God will do for them —and there have been a number of striking healings. A sadness is experienced when there are those who cannot quite believe that God wants them to be whole and therefore do not experience the healing that could take place.

The persons involved in the project feel it is important to help strengthen the faith of the close family members. There is a ministry at home following hospital visiting hours. Most of those who come to Pittsburgh hospitals are too sick to be cared for in their community hospitals, and the whole experience is often quite difficult if not tragic for the accompanying family members. To return each night to the four bare walls of a rented room can be terrifyingly lonely to one already filled with fear and grief. But in the Brethren homes—over a cup of coffee—the host and hostess can listen to and share the problems, can love them, pray with them and perhaps cry with them.

Most of the guests have returned home with a testimony of God's love and his healing power, and so His name is glorified. But the most pleasant surprise of all has been that those in the Pittsburgh Church have received more blessings than anyone else. Indeed, did not Jesus promise, ''. . . he shall not lose his reward''? (Matthew 10:42b)

A few days after Christmas of 1966 we received an urgent call from a distant pastor. A young man named Bill had been struck by a drinking driver while changing a flat tire along the highway. His legs had been crushed between the two cars, and his kidneys were failing from the shock. One of our Pittsburgh hospitals possessed

67

the only operative kidney machine within hundreds of miles. Bill's wife needed housing.

That young man was close to death when he arrived. We began to pray earnestly for him. He improved slightly. Suddenly his condition deteriorated until there appeared to be no hope remaining. Again we called people to pray. I knew in my heart that Bill would die unless we found more people who would pray. A minister had told me once about a non-denominational prayer group that met every Wednesday morning in Mount Lebanon, a Pittsburgh suburb. On Tuesday evening I called Elizabeth Gethin—"Tibb"—in whose house the meeting is held, to request prayer for Bill. She invited us to come to the meeting.

I announced to Norma, "We're going to a prayer meeting in Mount Lebanon tomorrow morning."

"Well, you might be; but I'm not!"

"Bill is going to die unless we get more people praying for him. We're going!"

Next morning I said, "Get ready. We're going to the prayer meeting."

"But look at my hair! I'm not interested in any self-righteous prayer group." Norma still had an unresolved grudge against God.

"You'd better get ready, because we are both going!" Norma began to cry. "Now don't start that! Just think how red your eyes will appear. Besides, Bill is dying!"

Finally she got the message. Sullenly Norma walked in Tibb's front door with me. I saw all those women, perhaps sixty of them—and I was ready to walk out. The instant Norma walked in,

68

she felt enveloped in love—and she was ready to stay.

The group prayed for Bill at the beginning of the service. Then we experienced a prayer meeting with a quality we had never before seen. Next Wednesday Norma asked, "Are you ready to go to Tibb's yet?"

"Well, I don't think we need to go. Bill is improving and . . ."

"I think we should go."

This is my wife? It's a miracle! Off we went to enjoy another feast.

The next week I left for Chicago to attend an eleven-day seminar for twelve Brethren ministers, all of whom had attended school together eight years before. As I tried to share with my former classmates what God had been doing in our Church, all but a couple merely spit it back at me. A God who acts was offensive to most of them. I thought, "Do these fellows actually pretend to be serving Jesus Christ?" The seminar was a humanistic, group-dynamics session. During those eleven days all my old personality aberrations were thrown in my face. And it hurt.

I returned to Pittsburgh discouraged. "Lord, why can't I witness for you so that people will listen? There's got to be more to the Christian life. There's got to be more to the pastorate. I'm tired of pushing."

I returned home to a blessing. While I was away one of our young mothers had needed rather immediate surgery. Two laymen quickly went to the hospital, anointed her and prayed for her. The next morning it was discovered on the operating table that the condition had totally disappeared. Oh, how good it was to be back where something meaningful was happening!

The next Wednesday we went to Tibb's and the following week also. Bill took another nosedive. The telephones began to ring through our congregation *and* through Tibb's prayer group. Again the Holy Spirit pulled Bill back from the very shore. Eventually we rejoiced to hear that Bill was able to return to his old job.

The fifth Wednesday at Tibb's led to eating lunch with Ruby. By this time Norma was starving, but not for physical food. I told Ruby about Norma's spiritual condition; Norma passively acknowledged what was being said. I ended with these words: "You take her; I am not the one to lead her to Jesus."

Ruby and Tibb kept Norma all afternoon. I was so excited I couldn't concentrate on my work. I picked her up at five and we drove home. Norma walked in the house and burst into tears. "I don't know why I'm crying. I'm so happy!"

Four days she cried. The children wanted to know what was wrong with Mother. "Not a thing," I told them with a grin. "Not a thing." On the fifth day the tears eased up, and Norma was able to resume her usual activities. By the end of one week the Holy Spirit had completely washed away her heartaches and hostilities. For Norma had been washed clean by the blood of the Lamb.

She had always been a good wife and mother, but we had not been walking together with the Lord. Norma was my best sermon critic: she knew instinctively the message I would be trying to get across. She just didn't believe it in her own heart.

We went back to Tibb's on Wednesday, where I gave a testimony of thanks to God for Norma's salvation, while she sat there and cried. And everyone loved her.

Bob and Doris are long-time friends. Doris had deep-seated emotional problems. Repeatedly I counseled her and finally sent her to a very competent psychiatrist. Hundreds of dollars later, he reminded Doris that she was fully aware of all her problems, yet she was no better. He suggested that she terminate the therapy. In despair Doris came to me. Contritely I told her to do what I should have suggested years before. She came with us to Tibb's prayer meeting and within an hour was a new creation. Jesus set her free. Since that day Bob also has experienced several miracles of healing in his body, including one when he was very nearly dead.

One day after Tibb's meeting there was special prayer, with the individual laying-on of hands. As we were preparing to leave, Maxine stood in front of me, put on a big smile and said, "Russ, you're ready for the baptism in the Holy Spirit."

I backed off slightly. Two thoughts came in rapid succession: "I've been making the wrong kind of friends! Does she think she's got something I don't have?" So I answered, "Do you mean the speaking-in-tongues?"

"Well-uh—, that's part of it." From my knowledge of the Bible I knew that "tongues" was not a valid objection, because the tongues was an integral part of the biblical experience. I was both curious and suspicious. A minister's wife moved in and within five minutes talked me out of five dollars for two tickets to a Full Gospel Business Men's dinner. I wasn't too difficult to sell.

IX. *The Power Flows*

We attended the Full Gospel Business Men's dinner with misgivings. Norma was apprehensive. So much had already happened to her in the previous two months that she felt unable to bear any more. I attended largely out of genuine curiosity. I wasn't afraid: I had brought my "sword" with me (Ephesians 6:17). Hadn't I been urging our congregation to judge by the scriptures, not by feelings? My head was crammed full of biblical theology. If that speaker says anything unbiblical, I'll use my "sword" on him. I observed quite a number of Mennonites present. This rather surprised me. After all, the Mennonites are quite similar to the Church of the Brethren. Jim Brown, a well-known Presbyterian pastor, was the speaker. As he spoke I merely waited. Sooner or later he'll say something unbiblical; then I'll know that this "baptism in the Holy Spirit" is not for Christians.

He never said it. In one hour of speaking, Jim said nothing unbiblical. He did not know me nor did he see me, but he snatched my own "sword" and hit me over the head with it. I was like a sitting duck, absolutely without defense. After the meeting someone asked, "Would you like to receive the baptism?"

Out came a stammered, "Yes." Looking at Norma to ask if she would join me, I noticed that her eyes appeared glassy. I took her hand, and she walked passively behind me to the front of the jammed banquet hall. I have discovered since how enormously popular Jim Brown is, yet with only a few minutes' wait he came walking over to meet us. The crowds seemed to disappear, and he was available.

Jim interpreted the baptism in the Holy Spirit for Norma and me. I began wondering, "Where have I been all these years? Why hasn't someone told me before?"

As we stood there, Jim hesitated and said to Norma, "Wouldn't you like to sit down?" Two chairs were placed behind us. I sat down. As Norma sat down her body went limp, and she slid gracefully to the floor.

"What hit her?" I wondered. "I didn't feel anything." Norma spent twenty minutes on that restaurant floor while Jim continued to talk to me. Then he prayed for us and left. Norma was still on the floor.* Several of our new friends tried to encourage me to pray in tongues, but I felt nothing, I heard nothing, I had nothing to say, and apparently the Holy Spirit had nothing to say through me.

A local pastor invited a group of us to his house following the meeting. Our hostess tried to do what she could for Norma, who could still barely

* Compare the experience of Saul of Tarsus, Acts 9:4.

74

sit and almost had to be put to bed. Norma was being filled with great love and tremendous power by the Holy Spirit. Yet I felt nothing. We had refreshments, talked and prayed for a long time.

As we prepared to go home—it was nearly two a.m.—I began to giggle. Soon everything anybody said would cause me to laugh. A feeling of love, deeper than any I had ever felt, oozed into my heart. I loved everybody in that room! In saying goodbyes, I embraced the other men and even picked up a Presbyterian minister's wife and hugged her! This was so unlike me, with all my reserve and shyness. We drove home and went to bed.

Next morning—Saturday—we were rudely awakened by one of our boys. "Daddy! Mother! The commode is running over!" Norma dashed to the bathroom to discover water flowing all the way out onto the carpet in the hall. We had discovered the problem on Friday evening but hadn't time to fix it before leaving for the dinner. So we had left instructions for our four children to use the downstairs lavatory. That morning five-year-old Harold forgot. So Norma quickly gathered every rag and towel she could locate and soaked up the water, then went downstairs to prepare breakfast.

Perhaps this story sounds too intimate for the reader, but God usually deals with us in intimate ways. A casual reading of many parts of the Bible reveals a great frankness.

After the excitement died and everyone else

had gone downstairs, I entered the bathroom to brush my teeth. As I was brushing I prayed, "Lord, why do I feel so joyful yet have not been able to speak in tongues? Did I really receive the baptism in the Holy Spirit last night?"

Immediately I heard that voice which had been silent since seminary days. For the third time in my life He spoke: "Put me to the test."

As I marvelled at hearing the voice again I asked, "How?"

The voice said, "Flush the commode."

"Just a minute!" I thought. "Is this the Holy Spirit or is this Satan?" I continued to brush my teeth.

Again He spoke: "I said, Flush the commode!" There was a note of insistence.

I looked at the damp floor, at the spot on the hall carpet, and said, "Nothing doing!"

"I said, Flush the commode!" Urgency was the note this time. I thought of the flood we had already seen. I thought of how irritated—justifiably so—Norma would be if I added another overflowing when I knew better. I put up my toothbrush, stepped over to the commode and said, "I just can't do it!"

"Flush the commode!" came the fourth time, and this command sounded highly impatient. An idea popped into my mind. I looked for all the wet rags and towels to place about the commode. Then I would flush it.

But Norma had taken every cloth to the basement and had put them in the washer. I had no safeguards, no earthly protection. I placed my hand on the handle and drew it back. Again I tried and couldn't do it. At last, praying, "Lord, this had better be from you," I pushed the handle down and jumped back from the inevitable overflowing. The water came up and up—almost to the top. As I put my hands to the sides of my head and said, "Oh, no! Here it comes!" the water suddenly shot down the drain as if a giant hand had thrust it down.

I stood there in disbelief. There came a little chuckle, then a laugh. Within seconds I was doubled up with laughter. And I laughed most of my waking hours for the next two weeks.

Never had I felt such overwhelming joy. I walked through the house, through the church, up and down the stairs, laughing hilariously. I laughed away a lifetime of heartaches. Saturday night exactly two weeks later I prepared for bed. I was talking and laughing. I stopped abruptly and looked at Norma. She was huddled at the top of the bed, trying to stay as far away from me as possible. A new thought occurred to me. I said, "You're afraid of me, aren't you?"

"Who wouldn't be—the way you've been roaming all over the house, laughing and praising God?"

"I'm sorry. I've been so high I was unaware that it frightened you." And we had our first intimate talk since receiving the baptism in the Holy Spirit. For just as the Holy Spirit gave me a totally opposite personality, He did the same for my wife. During these two weeks Norma had been unusually quiet and reserved. For a long period she was reluctant to pray in tongues, although she could do so very easily.

She went on to explain the difficulty of living with me. "I've been married to three different men in less than twenty years. I can't change husbands so fast without some time to adjust." I knew she was right. The fellow she married was without salvation. Then, upon his salvation, she had to adjust to a "new creation." All of a sudden he was filled with the Holy Spirit, and this change was at least as profound as the new birth. While I was eager to move with the Spirit, Norma was hesitant for the first several weeks.

Tongues however came more slowly to me than Norma. Eight days after receiving the baptism I was seated at my desk. The Lord had just given me my entire sermon in four short hours. I leaned back in the swivel chair, thanking Him for this gift. (Normally I needed days to develop a sermon.) As I looked up I seemed to see a blackboard. Words in English letters began moving across that blackboard. I read out loud what I saw—and the vision disappeared. Quickly I grabbed paper and pen and wrote down the words. They appeared to be a single sentence from some East African dialect. How unconventional God is! Such a curious means of presenting His gift of praying in the Spirit!

I leaped from the chair to tell Norma. She was relatively unimpressed. But I laughed and laughed. That day—the eighth day of my two-week laughing "jag"—my ribs became so sore I could hardly breathe.

Several other physical reactions followed the baptism. I had been overweight, perhaps ten pounds more than I wished. Within ten days the Holy

Spirit took off nine pounds and in subsequent weeks He removed two or three more pounds. That excess weight has never returned. All my physical reactions were heightened. He made me sensitive to physical stimuli such as I had never known before. Food tasted better, the bed felt better, I could see the world around me more clearly, all my physical senses were sharpened. The Holy Spirit really "turned me on." I had been living only half a life. Surely fear and hostility had been robbing me of much of the good pleasure God has placed in this world. Several weeks later I celebrated my fortieth birthday, and I am firmly convinced that life does indeed begin at forty!

Thus went my earliest days of this walk in the Spirit. But what did He do for my ministry to others?

That too was affected instantly. Before we received the baptism that Friday night, I had already completed my Sunday sermon. So it was probably an ordinary sermon. Sunday morning I gave an invitation to come forward for prayer at the end of the service, and the entire front of the Church was quickly filled with people. Many who didn't come forward were quietly weeping at their seats. A number of hearts were changed that morning.

But I had said nothing unusual. The Holy Spirit did the work, as He demonstrated later that same day. I had been invited to preach for community Holy Week services in a nearby county that Sunday evening. Feeling so elated over the response to the morning service, I repeated the same sermon that night. It fell flat. My first hard lesson came quickly.

Nothing however could take away my enthusiasm for Jesus Christ. I continued to preach Him every Sunday, and occasionally the Holy Spirit would fall and great changes would take place in various members of the Church. Attendance increased. Different people would comment on the "magnetism" pulling them to the front of the Church upon an invitation.

Still, I knew what I had formerly felt about the speaking-in-tongues. I had been certain in my heart that people who spoke in tongues were ignorant, uninhibited and emotionally unstable. The great procession of prominent individuals coming into this experience today of course belies that opinion. But my earlier feelings caused me to maintain silence about the tongues around other people. Norma and I would not share our experience with anyone in the congregation. We wanted to—desperately. But we felt that the shock would be too great, and the Holy Spirit seemed to concur.

Then one Wednesday a lady from our congregation asked for prayer at Tibb's. As the other women prayed for her, they asked the Lord to baptize her in the Holy Spirit. Olive got out of the chair and for a week, as she later described it, felt so oddly wonderful. Olive's heart was open though she had had no instruction whatever. Ten days later we asked Harold and Olive to stop by our house. We began to explain what was happening to her and then asked Harold if he would like to receive the same experience. "Well," he replied, "it sure has made her easier to live with." We all laughed and we prayed. And then we were four.

So it began. One- or two-at-a-time our members quietly received the filling with the Holy Spirit. A silent revolution was beginning to remake the congregation, a revolution activated and empowered by God's own Holy Spirit.

One Sunday evening a young man came to the Prayer Service for the first time. He came with a purpose. I had spoken to his wife perhaps too forcefully about accepting Jesus Christ. Their first child had been born without a right arm, and the memory of this tragedy was still an open wound in the mother's heart. So Ron came that Sunday evening specifically to let their pastor know that he had gone too far in counseling Judy. But the young man never had the opportunity to speak his mind, for the Lord baptized him in the Holy Spirit before he could register his complaint. Ron left the Church wondering what had hit him.

Within weeks Judy accepted her salvation and was also filled with the Holy Spirit. Shortly after, they found themselves expecting again. Judy grew more and more apprehensive. Would this child be normal? The tension was increasing. One night as she lay in bed in great distress, the Holy Spirit gave Ron a prophecy, in which He promised a healthy baby. The remaining six months were weeks of joyful anticipation as Ron and Judy received by faith the perfect little son they could not yet see.

X. *Everywhere I Turn*

Within a matter of days after being baptized
in the Holy Spirit, I began to realize that miracles
would sometimes happen if I merely came around.
People would ask leading questions about God—
questions almost no one would ask me before.
Strangers in need of prayer would appear spontaneously. A despondent Christian would be laughing after I had been there. Healings would take
place almost behind my back. A smile—now very
nearly a permanent part of my face—quickly replaced the sober countenance built out of forty
years of heartaches. I like what someone has eloquently said, ''If you're happy in the Lord, why
not let your face know about it!'' The Holy Spirit
has used that smile in some surprising ways.

No longer did I delude myself about why these
things were happening. In every case the Holy
Spirit was doing the work. The ''before'' and the
''after'' will ever remain a conspicuous contrast in
my memory. Often I hesitate to tell of my involve-
ment in these supernatural events, but God has
told me to relate boldly all stories in which He has
acted. They glorify His name and His power.

Six weeks after we were filled with Spirit, I

invited a friend to give a brief testimony to our congregation following my sermon. When he finished I gave an invitation for prayer. By prearrangement Norma and I also knelt at the front of the church and asked this layman to pray for us. I announced to the congregation that the two of us were promising God publicly that we would go anywhere He directed and do anything He asked.

Goldie was seated in the choir. For weeks she could "hardly put one foot in front of the other." The doctor was concerned about her increasing blood pressure. Her legs were swelling more and more each week. That Sunday morning there was a "pulling" sensation across her chest. Goldie said to herself, "Well, if I'm going to die, I'll die on the right side of the fence!" She came out of the choir to give her life to Jesus Christ. As this layman's hands touched her head she was struck by a charge of electricity which shot through her body. And Goldie had a brand-new heart, given by a God who loves her.

Two additional healings occurred that morning. How we thanked God for His powerful display of concern for our needs! Several others gave their lives to Jesus that day. Norma and I are convinced that God was also showing that He would honor our own faithfulness. He desires obedient servants.

About that time a neighboring Church of the Brethren pastor called on the telephone, inquiring as I answered, "How are you?"

I replied, "Man, I'm having a ball!"

He added later, "You're having a 'ball,' but I'm having a 'bawl'!" As with so many sincere pastors, he was having a difficult and discouraging time.

How my heart ached for him! But it still seemed premature to speak openly of the baptism in the Holy Spirit. Norma and I prayed for him. A few months later the Lord said abruptly that it was time to tell this pastor. I went to him and told him frankly, expecting a tongue-lashing. To my surprise he exclaimed, "Praise the Lord! I've been studying about the baptism for two years! I want that experience too!" He got it. The Lord appeared to him in the night, waking him from sleep. Thereafter the tongues would flow as this pastor prayed.

Pleasant little surprises are common in this life in the Spirit. Three months after receiving the baptism we heard that the Methodist Church one block up the street was getting a new pastor. Someone told me his name and I planned to visit him. But the weeks passed and the visit never materialized. At last, just before we left on vacation, I phoned. There was no answer. Later I tried again. Still no answer. So we departed on our vacation. As soon as we left, the mailman delivered some of our mail erroneously to the Methodist Church. The new pastor took the opportunity to meet me. He brought the mail personally, but we were already gone.

One week of our vacation was spent at a "Camp Farthest Out" in Maryville, Tennessee.

Ninety ministers were present. As the ministers met separately the first day, we stood up to introduce ourselves. Suddenly I heard a man give his name and his church in Pittsburgh. It was the neighboring Methodist minister, and we had come six hundred miles to meet each other! Our prayer group leader commented, "Isn't that just like the Lord!"

God gave us as mutual gifts to each other. At that very time we both had a great need which only the other could fill. For he too had been filled with the Spirit and was quite hungry for fellowship.

With the baptism in the Holy Spirit I was introduced to the authority of "the name of Jesus Christ." How the Father responds when we make requests in the name of the One to whom has been given all authority in heaven and on earth! (Matthew 28:18). What a difference that knowledge has made in praying against evil powers! Quite often we see demon-possessed persons set free from bondage by the authoritative stand on the name of Jesus Christ. Oh yes, I do believe in evil spirits now. We have dealt with many of them. We discovered that with the baptism in the Holy Spirit, Satan decides that his undercover game is no longer effective. He began to reveal himself in all his ugliness. After receiving some hard blows from him, we learned to depend on the power behind Jesus' name. In Him, we found, is our protection.

And the healings flowed as continual gifts from God. One of our ladies had a growth in her throat. As it grew larger with each passing month,

she was becoming terrified, but refused to see a
doctor. I encouraged her to seek medical attention,
but she was adamant. She simply would not face
the ominous possibilities. So I proposed what was
for her a radical course. She permitted several of
us to lay hands on her and pray for her. God
healed not only the growth, but a bursitis condition
of years' standing.

Barbara was in an automobile accident. Her
neck was broken, but the Xrays had not been made
properly, so that the break went unnoticed for
some days. We prayed for her continually as she
remained within a tiny fraction of an inch of permanent paralysis or even death. Her first baby was
due in two months. One day Norma and Tibb were
praying for Barbara, when the Holy Spirit told
Tibb that she was healed. All that night Barbara
suffered intense pain. But with the dawn the pain
in her neck was gone. After several weeks of frantic
searching, the mystified doctors pronounced her
healed. And a lovely baby girl came on schedule—
in perfect condition.

Charlie is one of our oldest members. He was
out-of-town, visiting his son, a doctor, when he suffered a serious heart attack. We kept the telephones
busy around the congregation, praying for Charlie.
His condition was listed by the hospital 250 miles
distant as gradually worsening. One morning a
nurse was taking his blood pressure when Charlie
felt the power of God slip through his right arm,
across his chest, and through the left arm. He was
healed and he knew it. The nurse quietly and quite
professionally stepped out of the room. Within two
minutes the room was full of doctors and hospital

personnel. What reading the Holy Spirit made on that dial we will probably never know.

A Church of the Brethren pastor called long-distance one evening. One of his members was in a Pittsburgh hospital. This was his third trip here for cancer, and his doctor had frankly told him that he was in the hospital for the last time. His pastor asked, "Russ, would you go cheer him up?" Walking in the room next day, I was greeted by the most disheartened couple I ever saw. He was dying, and neither he nor his wife held any hope. We began to discuss God's healing promises, and I noticed the dismal expressions change first to quizzical frowns, then to hopeful glances at each other and finally to smiles of confidence in God. The scriptures are faith-builders, and I was seeing them operate before my eyes. We prayed together, and he was discharged from the hospital two days later. No malignancy could be found in his body.

I had always been quite ill at ease in a hospital room. With no sympathy to give except an abiding hatred of sickness, I felt helpless. I have difficulty covering up my feelings with a professional pastoral countenance. After the baptism in the Holy Spirit I began to make hospital calls with eagerness, even with a longing—just to get my hands on the patient's head. Some of the greatest joys I experience come in hospital rooms. How I thank God for His willingness to heal!

The old periods of depression went out when the Holy Spirit came in. I have almost forgotten what it used to be like. For that same joy seems to bubble within even at difficult times. Now I understand how Paul could write from prison, exclaiming, "Rejoice in the Lord always!"

Perhaps more notable than the individual healings is the state of divine health that has been gradually developing within our congregation. I make many hospital calls, but seldom to visit any of our members. When Jesus Christ is exalted, good things begin to happen. The healing power of the Holy Spirit seems to reside within the four walls of the church. Even unbelievers, if they will attend services regularly, will find their health improved. This has been clearly demonstrated by several who discontinued their attendance at our church for various reasons. Old sicknesses began to show up in a rather brief time.

The Holy Spirit has given me a "front-door ministry." While folks are leaving the church following Sunday morning services, I stand at the door as is customary to shake their hands and ask, "How are you today?" If there are any problems, I lay hands on them and pray briefly. The Holy Spirit has done a number of miracles at that spot.

One day I was reminded by another minister of the marginal translations of Isaiah 53. My curiosity aroused, I opened the Hebrew Bible and began laboriously to translate verses 3–5. How different from the conventional versions! I took the translation back to my former professor of Hebrew; he made one notable correction and then pronounced it accurate. Apparently our translators hadn't the courage to deliver the message as received by them. While there are legitimate grounds for possible variations, the basic message is clear. The King James, the American Revised and the Revised Standard versions did violence to Isaiah's "Suffering Servant" with their weakened translations. For these verses declare unequivocally that our inheritance in Jesus Christ includes not only deliverance from sin but healing for our diseases. Here is the translation.

He was despised and forsaken by men,
 a man of pains and acquainted with sickness;
and as one who hides his face from us
 he was despised and we did not appreciate him.
Surely our sicknesses he has carried,
 and our pains he has suffered.
As for us—we have regarded him as one who was made
  ill,
 struck down by God and injured.
But he—he was wounded for our disobedience;
 he was afflicted in place of our punishment;
the discipline required for our wholeness was placed
  upon him,
and by his bruises we received healing within us.

God has given me a ministry of carrying that translation wherever I go. I seldom fail to introduce it. Anyone can then make the logical deduction that his healing was given to him 2,000 years ago. All he must do now is claim it by faith. Many have.

Ministers (of all people!) began a steady procession to our door for help. Always privately. I

90

could understand why the prominent religious teacher Nicodemus came to Jesus at night. I had explained about the baptism in the Holy Spirit to one minister and his wife, and they became, not surprisingly, defensive. So I let the matter drop. One day the Spirit told me to invite this couple to our house for the evening. Everything worked out. My schedule was clear and so was theirs. A baby sitter was available too.

So they came. Norma and I had fully intended to discuss the Holy Spirit; but after they arrived, the Spirit told both of us individually not to mention Him, but rather to make small talk all evening. How odd an instruction! But we each obeyed, not knowing that the other had received similar guidance.

Within a couple hours this minister and his wife were in a state of complete frustration. For each of them, unknown to the other, had compiled before they came a written list of objections to the baptism. And we were refusing to discuss the subject, even when they frantically brought it up.

Finally we went to the kitchen for refreshments. Norma suggested that we hold hands around the table as I began to give thanks for the food. During the prayer the Holy Spirit fell on the minister's wife. She told Jesus in the most moving terms how she loved Him, and the tongues poured from her lips. Her wide-eyed and startled husband became so envious and hungry that within several weeks he too received a baptism perhaps as dramatic as ours had been.

Some weeks after being filled with the Holy Spirit, God began to tell us that He was making a chapel of our livingroom. On faith we ordered new furniture to replace all that was literally falling apart. The next day we received a check for one hundred dollars from someone who was almost a total stranger. And the Lord has indeed made a chapel of our livingroom. It has been the scene of many repentant tears, joyful exclamations and healing miracles.

One day a young couple came to the church to receive the baptism in the Holy Spirit. Although there are no accidents with God, another of our young women, seemingly accidentally, also became involved in the prayers. No one but the Holy Spirit knew quite how she happened to be present. This was a demon-possessed woman, with at least a suicidal spirit and perhaps others also. As the Holy Spirit filled her, the evil spirit threw her on her back and came out in the weirdest screams. Frightening perhaps, but she was free thereafter.

Finally one bubble burst. Month-after-month our members' health improved, and we had continued two-and-a-half years without a death. At last our oldest member, who had lived out-of-town for a year-or-more, graduated to meet the Lord he loved. Shortly after, a chronically-ill lady who hadn't attended services in several years died at 84, the youngest in four years.

God's healing desires can be demonstrated clearly right in our home. All four of our children, down to six-year-old Johnny, know instinctively to lay hands on one another and pray for the Lord's healing. Although we have had no serious illnesses, He has healed us of many minor ailments as we pray for each other. The two oldest, seventeen-year-old Kathy and twelve-year-old Paul, have both been filled with the Holy Spirit according to His wise timing. We know too that the two youngest boys will receive in God's own schedule.

We have discovered also that as Jesus Christ is proclaimed in a steady diet, a deepening of the love and fellowship occurs within the congregation. A concern for one another is apparent. Visitors repeatedly note these qualities. Spirit-filled Christians who continue to grow are given new compassion for the suffering and the lonely. Our members are touching many lives outside the congregation.

Has there been resistance to the Holy Spirit within our Church? Definitely. But exactly a year after we had been filled with the Spirit, a prophecy was given to me through a visiting minister. Although it was lengthy, the heart of the prophecy, which someone happened to be recording, gave this assurance:

"My son, people will say certain things. In fact, you've [already] found that they are bluffing. They will threaten. It's the work of the enemy. He would come against you through other people. But remember this, that I am greater than all that would oppose you. Rejoice in Me and go forward, declaring My Gospel in its fullness, and see the results that follow. For My Spirit shall lead the way and clear the path, and those that would be determined to stay in the path shall be

93

cut down on the right and on the left, for I am going to march forward as you march with me."

Indeed. The Lord had already demonstrated the prophecy several months before I heard it. One member heard stories about people in our congregation speaking in tongues, so he set out on a one-man crusade to stamp out this foolishness. Within six weeks the Holy Spirit healed him of a chronic ailment and literally knocked him to the floor. Three weeks later he was speaking in tongues. Saul of Tarsus seems quite contemporary!

The rest of the opposition has been primarily vocal. We humans are so easily misled by our opinions, by hearsay and by half-truth! But God's word is powerful and His truth inevitably is revealed. All of us who have been filled with the Spirit have made mistakes. This is a new experience for everyone. We are experimenting. Clever as he is, Satan makes all the profit he can from every mistake. Still—I am trusting God, resting in the faith that the words of His prophet spoken nearly two years ago are true and trustworthy. Thus far those words have come true.

A district executive in the Church of the Brethren was told that I had received the baptism in the Holy Spirit. His immediate comment was, "Well, Russ Bixler had better stay where he is. No other church in our denomination would have him now!" Yet in the first two years after being filled with the Spirit, I was offered more pastorates than in all the previous years combined. How faithful God is!

Each Christmas we hold an "open house" for the congregation following the Sunday morning service. One December we had a series of unusually heavy bills and were running close on our expenses. There was a balance of $32 in the checking account with which to buy food for our guests. On Tuesday morning before the open house I sat down at my desk and noticed a couple newsletters from friends who were operating faith missions. I said, "Well, we hardly have enough money for the open house, so we can't help them." I threw the top letter in the wastebasket. As the paper touched bottom the Holy Spirit spoke: "Take that letter out of there and give him a contribution!"

"But Lord, we don't have enough now!"

"I know it." And that ended the conversation.

I pondered the matter a few minutes before going home to get the checkbook. As I wrote "$5" on the check stub, He spoke again: "No! Double it!" I swallowed hard and changed the figure to "$10."

Then He spoke again: "Now give the other one a contribution."

"But Lord! We don't have enough now!"

"I know it."

The perspiration began to flow. I grabbed the checkbook and started to write another ten dollars on the stub, when He said, "No! I want it all! You are to walk by faith!"

By this time I was an emotional wreck. But I went ahead with a check for twenty dollars. Hastily mailing the two letters before losing courage, I ran into the church and fell on my knees.

95

"Father! You've got me out on a limb! In Jesus' name, don't saw it off!"

Then came a strong urge to read the Bible. I quickly returned to the study where I had been reading Isaiah. I felt like a suffering servant, so I decided to read that passage, which begins at 52:13. I normally use the Revised Standard Version, which is the version I was using when Jesus came into my life. Isaiah 52:13 begins thus in the RSV: "Behold, my servant shall prosper . . ." The words seemed to leap off the page! I began to laugh. I laughed until I cried. Within seconds I was able to concentrate on my work as if nothing unusual had happened.

Half an hour later a man walked in the front door. We knew each other, but not well. He had left his office in the middle of the morning to come. He said, "Merry Christmas! The Lord told me to give this to you!" and threw a check for one hundred dollars on my desk.

Several months ago the Lord was urging me to send another gift to the same mission to which I had given the twenty dollars. After His repeated gentle nudgings, I sat down to send a check for ten dollars. A strong feeling swept over me that ten dollars was not the proper amount. I asked Him, "Well, then, how much should it be?" Instantly a figure of $13.97 popped into my mind. I could even see the numbers. It seemed so odd that I felt constrained to accompany the check with an explanatory letter, requesting a reply to confirm or to confute my unusual guidance.

The recipients were puzzled until they found in their mail a notice from the power company that the electricity would be shut off if they didn't pay their overdue bill of $13.97. Somehow the original billing had been lost, and the Lord simply wanted to remind them that He was watching over the mission.

Norma and I had always walked together in the natural realm. Since the baptism we are closer than ever before because we are walking together in the same Spirit also. Each of us recognizes almost instinctively what the Lord is saying to the other, and we respect each other's guidance, no matter how strange it may seem at the moment. Repeatedly miracles have occurred because both of us were responding together to the leading of the Spirit. Such confirmations give us growing courage to act much more decisively. We are quite different in personality, yet the Lord uses the differences in such a way that we complement each other. Norma is not an ''assistant pastor,'' yet she is still greatly used by the Lord, even within the framework of her primary responsibilities as wife and mother.

Before the experience of salvation I had little concern for a sufferer. After the new birth the

Holy Spirit put a compassion in my heart; but
being powerless, I felt totally frustrated. Following
the baptism, the Holy Spirit deepened that compassion enormously—but not without the tools to
do something about it. The contrast was sharp.
It was He who made all the difference. When a
heart hungry for God comes near me, that same
divine compassion is aroused within me, so that I
am continually being reminded that Jesus Christ
is both the motivation and the answer.

Several times I have experienced complete
failure within hours after being used by God very
dramatically. Each time the Lord has told me,
"That's just to remind you that I am the One who
does the work and I alone am to receive the glory."
Those disasters have literally crucified any pride
left within me. Furthermore, I know with great
certainty that if I fail to give God the glory for
His work, I will suffer more of these deeply-embar-
rassing failures. As long as I maintain the proper
priorities, God continues to pour out His blessing.
Everywhere I turn He manifests His glory.

Lest there be misunderstanding of the baptism
in the Holy Spirit, I would never esteem this gift
as being as vital as the gift of salvation. Salvation
in Jesus Christ will always remain the crucial human need until Jesus returns. As wonderful as is
the baptism in the Spirit, it is intended only for
this life. "But you shall receive power when the
Holy Spirit has come up on you; and you shall be
my witnesses . . . to the end of the earth" (Acts

1:8). On the other hand, salvation is for all eternity. Then we will no longer need to be filled with the Holy Spirit, for we shall be with Jesus.

The difference in relative importance is spelled out by Jesus in Luke 10:19,20. "Behold, I have given you authority to tread upon serpents and scorpions, and over all the power of the enemy; and nothing shall hurt you. Nevertheless do not rejoice in this, that the spirits are subject to you; but rejoice that your names are written in heaven." The apostle Paul thanked God that He spoke in tongues more than all the Corinthians (1 Corinthians 14:18), yet his constant emphasis was the overriding need of salvation through the sacrifice of Jesus Christ. Being filled with the Holy Spirit gives a Christian, during the years of this life, the power to witness for Jesus Christ—with concrete results. The healings and other miracles are simply God's way of demonstrating His love and His power. Seldom is an unbeliever blessed by that healing power without a subsequent experience of salvation.

The speaking-in-tongues normally accompanies the baptism in the Holy Spirit, or at least follows it. Why?

First, this is the uniform biblical description of the experience. In each recorded case of receiving the baptism the believers spoke in tongues: Acts 2:4; 8:14–17 (implied); 10:44–46; 19:6. Tongues are usually words of praise, personal and devotional. Perhaps the phenomenon could be called more accurately the *"praying*-in-tongues." Occasionally in a group meeting the Holy Spirit will give someone a "message in tongues" which normally will be interpreted into the known language. Tongues and interpretation are two of the nine gifts of the Spirit (1 Corinthians 12:4–11). This latter manifestation is different from the initial reception of the Holy Spirit by a Christian, an experience which, according to the biblical norm, is always accompanied by the tongues.

I have noticed few "spiritually proud" persons receiving the Holy Spirit. To give up to the Holy Spirit the control of one's words requires a humility which is often quite painful emotionally. Perhaps the Lord wants a demonstration that He can trust us with His power, that we would be willing to give up to His Spirit a control that we have always reserved for ourselves.

At any rate the biblical experience has been fulfilled in my personal experience. I have always demanded that any "new" teaching be strictly biblical. The remarkable accuracy of the Bible, a fact which I had cautiously accepted on faith, is continually being demonstrated in actual experience.

Once I was lonely, caught between the fundamentalists and the liberals, somewhat uncomfortable in both camps. But now Jesus Christ has given me my family. I am at home in a Spirit-led Episcopal Church; I am at home in a store-front Pentecostal meeting. These are all part of the huge family God has given me. I stand in a good tradition, as demonstrated by Mark 3:31–35:

And his mother and his brothers came; and standing outside they sent to him and called him. And a crowd was sitting about him; and they said to him, "Your mother and your brothers are outside, asking for you." And he replied, "Who are my mother and my brothers?" And looking around on those who sat about him, he said, "Here are my mother and my brothers! Whosoever does the will of God is my brother, and sister, and mother."

XI. *Ever-opening Doors*

The Church of the Brethren was founded in Germany in 1708 by a group of Christians who were determined to follow Jesus Christ, come what may. Of course, when men's hearts are so open, the Lord will honor his servants with His Holy Spirit. Our church historians have a few limited records of the gifts of the Spirit being poured out among those earliest Brethren. But there were dissensions and some divisions occurred. Religious persecution fell heavily upon the Brethren and they were scattered, some to Holland, and others to America. Eventually those in Holland came to America also. Thus the Church of the Brethren, (or as it was once called, the German Baptist Brethren; a nickname was "the Dunkers") died out in Europe.

The early Brethren abhorred the creeds of the established churches. They agreed that they would have no creed but the New Testament. They attempted to follow the New Testament ordinances most literally. The Brethren have always practiced the full Love Feast (Jude 12), including the washing of one another's feet (John 13:1–17), the meal itself and of course the Eucharist. The Brethren would turn the other cheek when abused. They

103

practiced the anointing for healing and the laying-on-of-hands. The simple, unadorned life, non-swearing and other New Testament instructions were faithfully adhered to.

Through the generations these ordinances tended to become static traditions. The vitality was lost, and the Brethren began to turn in on themselves, due largely to wartime persecutions for their stubborn biblical pacifism. In recent years, however, the Church of the Brethren has turned toward the world, rejecting dead traditions, but also rejecting much that has value.

When I received the baptism in the Holy Spirit all the New Testament ordinances took on richer meanings. I find it much easier to wash another's feet, embrace him and give him the holy kiss (1 Thessalonians 5:26). The Holy Spirit has brought tradition to life. Whenever Brethren proclaim that "the New Testament is our rule of faith and practice," I feel like shouting "Amen!"

In 1958 we celebrated the 250th anniversary of the founding of the Church of the Brethren. A number of the modern Brethren made the journey to the little village of Schwarzenau, Germany, where the initial group of eight dedicated Christians had organized themselves. While these twentieth-century Brethren were there, some people from Denmark arrived. To their mutual surprise both groups were celebrating the same anniversary. Neither had known of the other during the 250 years. The persecution had apparently driven some of the Brethren to Denmark.

But the Danish Brethren were different. The gifts of the Holy Spirit have been in operation in that group throughout the years.

Some time after the Schwarzenau encounter one of the Danish Brethren came to the United States to visit the American Brethren. He was appalled at the lack of dedication to Christ! He cut short his visit and returned home heart-broken, locking himself in a room to pray and fast for the American Brethren for 21 days. At the end of the three weeks the Holy Spirit told him to remain there another full week, praying and fasting for the American Brethren. Twenty-eight days without food! I've been told that he came out of that room as strong as when he entered it. I know that I am one who has received great blessing from God as a result of my Danish brother's fasting and praying. How I praise the Lord for this faithful man I have never met!

For years we had attempted to have regular Sunday evening services in our Church. Every attempt inevitably dwindled to nothing. All through the years I knew God wanted us to have a Sunday evening service. But nothing seemed to work. The Sunday evening service is a dying institution in most American churches. A few weeks after the Holy Spirit moved into our lives He told me that the time had come. We announced briefly in the

Sunday bulletin, "There will be a Prayer Service in the Church at 7:30 p.m."

Several showed up. Every Sunday evening there was at least one person present besides Norma and me. Attendance slowly picked up as more received the Holy Spirit until the average was close to fifteen. By this time visitors from other churches were coming. We moved freely in the Spirit, while the Sunday morning service remained basically the same, a traditional Protestant worship service, except for occasional invitations as the Spirit led.

We couldn't find a pianist willing to play for the Prayer Service, so I blew the dust off my guitar and began to accompany the singing. I announced that the guitar would be put away as soon as we found a pianist. The guitar is still present, and I suspect that the folks wouldn't allow it to be replaced.

Attendance at the Prayer Service the second year averaged seventy-five in a room that is built for sixty. Normally the crowd bulges into the rooms at either end. Sometimes we are forced to move into the main auditorium which can seat 150. But there the informality and the sense of individual participation is dissipated.

While the members of our congregation normally are the largest group represented, there have been times when there were more Episcopalians or Presbyterians than Brethren. Once the largest single group was Roman Catholic. Miracles are regular occurrences in the Prayer Service. On occasion the testimony period has taken a full hour. Prophecy, tongues and interpretation are often given. Hundreds have received salvation and the baptism in the Holy Spirit. Last summer the meeting room was uncomfortably warm, so a frequent visitor placed this ad in her community newspaper.

Wanted—air conditioner needed by a beautiful little church that is doing so much for the Lord and his children.

The air conditioner came! When it proved too small, several sizable contributions were given to install a larger, adequate unit.

Our small congregation (150 members) has touched the lives of thousands in the Pittsburgh area. This ever-widening impact is just another aspect of "taking up our cross," complementing the Hospitality Project most appropriately. There is a precious balance of the physical and the spiritual in our service for Jesus Christ.

The "generation gap" is almost non-existent when the Holy Spirit is present. In fact, young people will usually move with the Spirit much more readily than older folks. The youth come out to the services because something real and powerful is happening. They like to be where the action is. After our teenage daughter received the baptism in the Holy Spirit, most of the high school youth followed her lead, one-by-one, into the same experience. Young people are simply seeking reality. They are unmoved by "playing church."

The Prayer Service is strengthened by recognizing the "body of Christ." As Paul says, "Now

107

you (plural) are the body of Christ and individually members of it'' (1 Corinthians 12:27). Each person is free to contribute whatever portion of the worship the Holy Spirit might give him. ''All these are inspired by one and the same Spirit, who apportions to each one individually as He wills'' (1 Corinthians 12:11). Following two hours of worship, testimony and prayer, we conclude the service only to begin the individual laying-on-of-hands, which may last two or three more hours. So much more power seems to be available when the ''body of Christ'' ministers to the needs of the one seated in the midst of the saints.

We have learned too the importance of praising God. The Pentecostals have known this for years, but we are newly discovering how the Lord honors His praises.

With the baptism in the Holy Spirit, doors began to open. After forty years of closed doors! Praise the Lord! I have been impressed by the interest and openness of Episcopalians, for many Episcopalian churches have invited me to speak. The Holy Spirit seems to work a little more powerfully through me in these particular services. Several years ago this would have seemed utterly impossible.

Five brief months after being filled with the Holy Spirit we attended a Saturday night prayer meeting in Jim Brown's Upper Octorara Presbyterian Church at Parkesburg, Pennsylvania. Seated behind us was the president of the Lancaster, Pa.,

Chapter of the Full Gospel Business Men's Fellowship. They had been unable to obtain a speaker for their October meeting, and the Holy Spirit had told him that their speaker would be present at the prayer meeting that night.

Jim called on me to give a brief testimony, which I did hesitantly, quite unsure of what I was supposed to say. I had never before given a personal testimony, but the Lord told the Chapter president, "There's your speaker."

After asking every Spirit-filled Christian I knew to pray for me—and I had every word of my story written long beforehand—I got up to speak at the Lancaster meeting. Glaring back at me was a very large Negro. Bob had been a professional basketball player and was now leading a Black protest move against the obvious racial discrimination in the plant where he worked. His greatest passion was a deep-rooted hatred of the white man and everything he represented. Bob had also toyed with the idea of joining the Black Muslims. And he glared at me—all the time I was speaking.

When the meeting was ended I invited the sick to come forward for prayer. The last man we prayed for was Preston, the precious Negro who had with difficulty persuaded Bob to attend. As we finished the prayer for Preston, the Holy Spirit told me, "Kiss him." I hesitated. Again He spoke, "Kiss him." So I planted a kiss on his cheek and we embraced. Preston was overwhelmed.

But Bob too had seen it. His entire philosophy of life came tumbling down like a house of cards. He had seen a white man kiss a black man. Bob not only accepted Jesus Christ as Lord but also was filled with the Holy Spirit in as exciting a baptism as I have ever seen. A violent man had to be dealt with violently by the Holy Spirit.

Bob's supervisor at the plant was a man of courage, unafraid to stand toe-to-toe with Bob—looking up to that giant of a man and calling him all the filthy names he could think of. Of course Bob had been answering the supervisor in the same manner. The morning after the Chapter meeting Bob went to work early—he had been up all night in prayer—and walked straight to the supervisor's desk. He seized the supervisor's right hand, clasped it tightly in his own hand and said, "Forgive me! Forgive me! Forgive me!"

The supervisor pulled his hand away and looked back in sheer terror. "What's the matter with you? Are you crazy?" And he ran down the hall.

Next August Bob and Rose and their two pretty daughters visited us for a weekend. They were such a blessing to our congregation! Bob spoke from our pulpit on Sunday morning. We held a dialogue sermon. At the close of the sermon period I asked him publicly, "Bob, is there anything that we as an all-white congregation can do about the racial problem?"

Bob chuckled. "Russ, there is no racial problem. There is only 'sin,' and Jesus Christ is the answer to sin."

And that was that.

Rose was as tiny and petite as Bob was big

and strong. She had been deaf in one ear since childhood and also had a chronic heart condition which caused her feet to swell uncomfortably. As we prayed together on Saturday night the Holy Spirit opened Rose's ear and on Sunday afternoon He healed her heart. That was quite a weekend!

Shortly after filling me with the Holy Spirit the Lord instructed me to organize a group of Spirit-filled ministers. We called a luncheon meeting and seventeen appeared, including several Pentecostals whom I had never met. Ever since that day those in attendance at our monthly ministers' luncheons have consistently averaged half-Pentecostal and half from the historic churches. The Holy Spirit is so ecumenical! The mailing list now totals 230.

We call ourselves the Interfaith Ministers' Fellowship. The Fellowship has already sponsored two well-attended seminars on the Holy Spirit where both budgets were in the thousands. Each time voluntary offerings covered all expenses with a few dollars left over. Now the Fellowship is planning a six-day "Charismatic Conference," which could well be the largest such gathering that has ever taken place. We are boldly going ahead with plans as the Holy Spirit leads the way. While the first two seminars hosted perhaps a thousand each, we are expecting a much larger response for the Charismatic Conference. For the Holy Spirit is moving into nearly every church in the Pittsburgh area. A number of churches contain

Spirit-filled Christians by the dozens. We are deeply grateful to God for His special touch on the Pittsburgh area.

During a Sunday evening Prayer Service in January 1969 a voice spoke to me: "Tell these people that I have given you a new car." I was speaking at that moment on another subject, and I pondered whether or not the unexpected message was from God. It seemed so self-centered. I felt uneasy.

So I didn't say it. For three weeks I pondered this isolated, out-of-context command. Should I have spoken? I asked the Lord, but He remained silent. Exactly 23 days later I was leaving a home about twelve miles distant. There was a steady drizzle of rain. As I slipped behind the steering wheel and closed the door, the voice spoke again, "You wouldn't tell the people that I had given you a new car, so now I'm going to take this one away from you."

Instantly filled with tension, I fastened the seatbelt tightly. I was certain that someone would slide on the wet street and demolish the car. The apprehension was almost agonizing for the twelve miles, but the trip was uneventful. "What is He going to do? When will He do it?" And I began to pray earnestly.

The Lord wasn't delayed in bringing His words to pass. Within a couple days my old car (which had been in good condition) began to fall apart! At least every other day something else would go wrong, until I cried out, "All right, Lord! I get the message! I'll get a new car!"

He directed me to a new car which the dealer had been unable to sell because of the unusual combination of optional accessories. The dealer sold the car at a price far below what I would have paid for another, and the accessories just suit me fine!

Slowly I am learning to listen to His voice. I am stubborn and I am hesitant to move in the Spirit because all the fear is not yet cleansed from my heart. But the Holy Spirit is gently working. In spite of my shortcomings in the area of simple, childlike trust, the Lord is still opening new doors for me. I have spoken in a number of places across the eastern half of the country. Doors continue to open in surprising places.

The miracles of healing have slowly fallen off among our congregation. This is as it should be when a condition of divine health settles upon a church. More of us are learning to appropriate the life of Jesus Christ within ourselves. More of us are discovering how to resist illness, and it shows. All this in spite of the statistical fact that illness has multiplied in the last century! Although medical science has made phenomenal strides since 1880, lost-time from work due to illness has proportionately multiplied three-and-a-half times. The proclamation of the Gospel of Jesus Christ in the full power of the Holy Spirit is the only cure!

Some months ago the Lord gave me the outline for a healing brochure. We selected 22 scriptures that contain God's promises to heal, and they were printed in a three-fold brochure. On the cover is a doctor's prescription blank, with the title, "The Great Physician Prescribes . . ." The prescription gives instructions to take the "medicine" four times a day.

Two days after the printer delivered the brochures, a friend stopped at our home for prayer. She had suffered for years from a hiatal hernia and a stomach ulcer, requiring a permanent diet of bland food. We prayed for her and gave her one of our new prescriptions to add to her collection of medicines. She took the new medicine faithfully for 48 hours. Suddenly the power of God fell upon her, surging like electricity through her body. That evening she sat down to her first full dinner in many years.

Within the first six months one printing of brochures was exhausted, and we are shipping out orders from the second printing. Both times we ordered the prescriptions with no money on hand, but God provided every penny. We knew it was in the will of God after the printer charged $135 for the first printing: by the time he delivered the order, $136 had been given to us. Accompanying the bulk orders for brochures is this statement:

> This prescription has been prayerfully compounded. If taken as directed, accompanied by faith in the prescribing Physician, the medicine is remarkably effective. Overdoses are not harmful, and permanent addiction is desirable.

Like our friend who enjoys her food once again, people in need call frequently to talk to

Norma or me about their problems. Indeed, we are nearly inundated by callers and visitors, but we are thrilled just to be used by the Lord in such supernatural ways. Prior to the baptism in the Holy Spirit I was full of advice. I had the answer for everyone's problem—but few came for help. I have long since stopped giving free advice. Now I merely point them toward Jesus and let the Holy Spirit tell them what to do.

XII. *God's Hand on the Future*

The morning prayer of the Pittsburgh Experimenter has always fascinated me: "Good morning Lord. I love you. What have you planned for today? I want to be a part of it."

Those are my feelings about the future. A thrilling aspect of the Holy Spirit's work is simply —tomorrow. The surprising adventures He has in store for those who will walk with Him! Some of the prophecies given to me by total strangers have been awesome. If these prophecies concerning my personal future prove to be as accurate as those already fulfilled, then perhaps my youthful dreams were not as extreme as they appeared, but only misdirected. Jesus is a pleasant "Boss," easy to work for. "Take my yoke upon you, and learn from me . . . For my yoke is easy, and my burden is light" (Matthew 11:29,30). Now my ambitions concern not what I desire, but what Jesus desires.

Still, there *is* something that I want very much. I want more of Jesus Christ. My personal search for truth has ended in Him. Yet the search is only beginning, for I will never in this life receive enough of the life of Jesus to satisfy me. I cannot stand still. And this is one of my problems, for there are times when the Lord merely wants me to rest in Him, to wait upon Him before I move ahead. He is teaching.

I especially want more of His love. With my idealism I never could accept a lie, a half-truth or even an exaggeration. Therefore, whenever someone confronts me with such, my initial reaction, as ever, is to want to reply with the truth. But a "caution light" flashes within. For the Lord has repeatedly reminded me that I reply with what I *think* is the truth and, being human, I too can be in error. Today He is teaching me to accept untrue accusations and return a smile, for Satan's chief weapon is the lie. Jesus is showing me how love can conquer any lie.

I must remember that an unbeliever is spiritually blind and deaf. He simply cannot see or hear until he permits the Holy Spirit to reveal the truth of Jesus Christ to him. How I, as a rather typical evangelical pastor, used to seek to persuade men of the Gospel by logic and argument! Words alone are not enough to convince. People also need to feel the love of Jesus flowing through me. Both the presentation of the Gospel and His love are necessary for effective witness (Ephesians 4:15).

Often I have pondered the possible reasons why some Christians grow so beautifully following the baptism in the Holy Spirit, and others stop growing the moment they speak in tongues. Worse yet, there are the inevitable few whose lives present a rather poor witness for the Holy Spirit. My own testimony is that the baptism in the Holy Spirit could be compared to a door which opens miraculously into a long hallway—an endless hallway—of earthly growth in Christ. This hallway is the path along which one maintains his daily "walk in the Spirit." It is a path leading toward "mature manhood, to the measure of the stature of the fulness of Christ" (Ephesians 4:13b).

Having counseled with hundreds of Spirit-filled Christians who are wondering why they are not growing as they would like, there seems to be a "checklist" of items, the absence of any one of which will result in a retardation of spiritual growth. I ask, "*First*, are you studying your Bible daily?" Depending upon the answer to that question before asking the next one, I follow with, "*Second*, do you spend time in prayer each day, including prayer in the Spirit (i.e., prayer in tongues)?" If the reply is again affirmative, the final question is, "*Third*, are you involving yourself in regular fellowship with other Spirit-filled Christians?"

Thus far I have found that every Christian who is troubled about his lack of growth in Christ will confess an inadequate discipline at one or more of these points. Indeed, this checklist was developed existentially—as the result of a prayerful examination of my own weaknesses and failures. It should prove helpful to the sincere reader.

Nearly fifteen years have passed since that night in the car when God first spoke. If I grow as much in the next fifteen years as—well, it's going to be exciting! I know Jesus is coming soon and that He is equipping His army for the final struggles. How honored I feel to be invited to take part! Just for now though, my abiding sense of accomplishment and deep satisfaction with life are continuing qualities of daily existence. My theme song comes from the youth presentation, "For Heaven's Sake." *

I'm nothing; I'm nobody; I'm no one;
But Someone made something of me.
And He put on my flesh and He walked in my bones,
And He saw all the grief that I see;
He saw all the grief that I see.

He knows what I know of tormentors—
That haunting and howling within,
And the blood I can spill and the bones I can break,
And the flesh with the nails driven in;
The flesh with the nails driven in.

He hung on the cross like a creature,
Wearing my sin-spattered clothes;
And the pride of my flesh died with Him when He died.
And my raiment was new when He rose;
My raiment was new when He rose.

This garment I wear with a difference;
'Twas flesh when the King entered in;
And He put there His love—yes, His almighty love,
And it never can be what it's been;
It never can be what it's been.

I'm nothing; I'm nobody; I'm no one;
I'm someone and Christ is in me;

* Words by Helen Kromer, North American Ecumenical Youth Assembly, 1961.

And I'll put on His flesh and I'll walk in His bones,
And a part of His body I'll be;
A part of His body I'll be.

The story is obviously unfinished. Thus far it is the story of how God can take a failure and use him.

It can happen to anybody!